T0369883

THE WHOLE WORLD'S WATCHING

THE WHOLE WORLD'S WATCHING

DECARBONIZING THE ECONOMY AND
SAVING THE WORLD

———————◆———————

MARTYN TURNER
and
BRIAN O'CONNELL

JOHN WILEY & SONS, LTD
Chichester • New York • Weinheim • Brisbane • Singapore • Toronto

Other Wiley Editorial Offices

John Wiley & Sons Inc., 605 Third Avenue,
New York, NY 10158-0012, USA

Wiley-VCH Verlag GmbH, Pappelalle 3,
D-69469 Weinheim, Germany

Jacaranda Wiley Ltd, 33 Park Road, Milton,
Queensland 4064, Australia

John Wiley & Sons (Asia) Pte Ltd, 2 Clementi Loop #02-01,
Jin Xing Distripark, Singapore 129809

John Wiley & Sons (Canada) Ltd, 22 Worcester Road,
Rexdale, Ontario M9W 1L1, Canada

British Library Cataloguing in Publication Data

A catalogue record for this book is available from the British Library

ISBN 0-471-49981-1

Typeset in 11/13.5pt Perpetua by Footnote Graphics, Warminster, Wilts.

Printed and bound by CPI Antony Rowe, Eastbourne

This book is printed on acid-free paper responsibly manufactured from sustainable forestation,
for which at least two trees are planted for each one used for paper production.

CONTENTS

FOREWORD

Any topic so loaded with economic and geopolitical significance as global warming is bound to bring heated differences of opinion. That's the way it has been in the USA, which has (rightly, both in my view and the view of the authors) declined to ratify the Kyoto Protocol on climate change. The USA has also found ways to use fossil fuels much more efficiently thanks to free-market ingenuity, and witnessed strenuous arguments over the cost in jobs, growth, and economic opportunity from artificial constraints on energy use as mandated by Kyoto. Kyoto's premise is that global warming is caused directly by carbon dioxide emissions: if that hypothesis is speculative, as I believe it is, we have to ask what kinds of costs we should be willing to bear to combat global warming, a phenomenon whose chain of causation is far from proven.

As Brian O'Connell and Martyn Turner make clear, the situation in Europe is far different than that in the USA, with global warming theory accepted as gospel and the costs of cutting carbon emissions universally approved. At least they *were* universally approved until this year's upsurge in fuel prices, which has conversely caused much more political turmoil in Europe than in America. That is not surprising, though, when we consider that Europe has a long tradition of both high fuel taxes and a higher tax burden than the USA overall. The reasons why global warming theory is taken as gospel in Europe are more complex. In part they stem from the iron linkage of non-governmental organizations and the

European governments, and in part from the central planning traditions that still plague many of our friends on the continent. Europe is also much more accustomed to a heavy regulatory hand, which makes it much more amenable to command-and-control energy policies. O'Connell and Turner do an excellent job of comparing the policy traditions of the USA and Europe in the course of making the case against Kyoto.

I do differ with the authors on one key point: they believe global warming is a real and important phenomenon, whereas I and my colleagues at the Competitive Enterprise Institute remain quite skeptical. Partly this is a semantic distinction, since virtually every analyst in the field of climate change agrees that the earth has warmed somewhere around one degree over the past century. What they don't agree on is the cause of that change, and so long as ground-based temperature measurements and satellite data give different results, I think skepticism remains the sounder position. Brian O'Connell and Martyn Turner do make a non-ideological, no-nonsense case for their view, however, and it is very much worth reading.

Whatever you may believe about global warming, no one disagrees that the private sector should have a keen interest in developing both new energy sources and ways to use energy much more efficiently. On this point O'Connell and Turner tell us much that we need to hear, including the prospect that entrepreneurs will succeed in developing a viable fuel cell technology to compete with fossil fuels, and the latent potential of nuclear energy to generate the power needed for the Internet Age. The authors have it exactly right: governments have never yet succeeded in revolutionizing technology, whether it involves energy exploration or fuel efficiency or power generation. Regulators can nudge things a bit at the margin, but they utterly lack the power of invention, innovation, and vision that lies at the heart of every technological breakthrough. That's the fundamental problem with Kyoto, which is dissected with great skill in *The Whole World's Watching*.

Yet there is an even more important point, one which O'Connell and Turner make with great force. It is this: whatever we as a society, through governmental or market measures, choose to do about climate change and energy use, we must ensure that the poor of the world do not pay the price. It's easy for third-way commentators to tell everyone to drive less and turn down the thermostat in pursuit of an abstract and questionable theory like global warming. It's quite another for them to pursue an agenda that would deny, or at least delay for many years, the economic and technological progress that has blessed us in the west with abundant energy, good jobs, life-saving medicines, and yes, the freedom to travel by automobile wherever we choose. However you feel about global warming there is no moral justification for denying the neediest people of the world the chance to climb the ladder of prosperity, freedom, and hope. And that, I'm convinced, is exactly what Kyoto would do.

On a personal note, let me say that *The Whole World's Watching* bears eloquent testimony to my long-held belief that the Kyoto Protocol is a manifestation of overwhelming arrogance on the part of third-way bureaucrats and their allies in interest groups, the media and, I'm sorry to say, much of the scientific community. Let us indeed have sound science and an open debate, but let us not prejudge the science of global warming based on sketchy and contradictory evidence, simply to justify putting the whole world's energy policies under the umbrella of a sweeping regulatory regime controlled by officials not directly accountable to the people of any nation.

Kyoto has set in motion a massive power struggle that will continue even when the specific treaty is dead and buried (as I believe it will be). That struggle is for power, not in the sense of controlling the world's energy sources but in the larger sense of gaining political power over who decides how fast the world economy should grow (or *if* it should grow), where future technologies will come from, and under what terms the peoples of the developing world will enjoy the blessings of economic freedom and the wealth they will derive therefrom. That wealth encompasses not just greater personal income, but also the quality of life – better healthcare, improved safety, a cleaner environment – that is the hallmark of an advanced free market economy. These are not issues for global authorities to decide, but for free peoples and their rightful governments to sort out on their own.

Brian O'Connell and Martyn Turner understand all of this and share their keen insights in *The Whole World's Watching*. Read it, and you will learn vital lessons about the forces shaping twenty-first century science, technology and politics. This is an important book.

JACK KEMP
Distinguished Fellow at the Competitive Enterprise Institute and
Co-director of Empower America
October 2000

JACK KEMP:BIOGRAPHICAL INFORMATION

Jack Kemp is a Distinguished Fellow at the Competitive Enterprise Institute (CEI), a Washington, DC-based public interest group dedicated to the principles of free enterprise and limited government. His work at CEI centers on promoting rational, free-market environmental policies, and raising awareness of international efforts to curb economic growth.

Mr Kemp is also a co-director of Empower America, a public policy and advocacy organization he co-founded in 1993 with William Bennett, Ambassador Jeane Kirkpatrick, Vin Weber, and Founding Chairman Ted Forstmann. Prior to 1993, he served for four years as Secretary of Housing and Urban Development.

Jack Kemp received the Republican Party's nomination for Vice President in August of 1996. In the previous year, Mr Kemp served as Chairman of the National Commission on Economic Growth and Tax Reform to study how major restructuring of the US tax code could help unleash the entrepreneurial spirit of Americans and grow the economy.

Before his appointment to the Cabinet, Mr Kemp represented the Buffalo area and Western New York for 18 years in the United States House of Representatives. He served for seven years in the Republican Leadership as Chairman of the House Republican Leadership Conference.

Jack Kemp came to Congress after 13 years as a professional football quarterback.

ACKNOWLEDGMENTS

We would like to thank in particular Myron Ebell at the Competitive Enterprise Institute in Washington, Emma Cornish at the Uranium Institute in London, Elena Nekhaev from the World Energy Council in London, Christopher van Halewyn from Prebon Energy Consulting Services in London, and Roland Hwang from the Union of Concerned Scientists in San Francisco. This book would not have been possible without timely data supplied by Wood Mackenzie, a division of Deutsche Bank AG. We would also like to thank Dina Turner for her comments and feedback while we were putting this book together.

1

THE WHOLE WORLD'S WATCHING

This book is all about solutions. It was not written for environmental-ists, but it was written out of concern for the environment. This is a book about money, and how to use it to solve a problem so grave that it is beyond a dollars and cents measurement. It is also a book that should inspire hope and reinstill confidence in mankind. It was written for anyone that wants to know how we can preserve the world in which we live for future generations without sacrificing the lifestyles we enjoy today. We do not envision an idealistic future where man lives in blissful harmony with nature, but we do recognize that a balance with nature has been lost and must be restored. This will happen by implementing solu-tions to the problem of global warming that we *know* work, and that will resolve, or at least delay, the threat of climate change. The environ-mentalists that first made us aware of the seriousness of the problem would not endorse many of the solutions we propose. Just because we share the same sense of urgency that they feel does not mean we think that they are best qualified to set the agenda for the future. We are capitalists, but we are also intelligent enough to know that free markets have to be shaped and managed for the good of all. The western world has at its disposal the skills and expertise of an industrial and financial machine that can be focused and motivated to solve almost any problem presented to it. We are at a crucial point in time where the process of preventing the threat of climate change has to begin. This book will explain how capitalism can be used to fix the problems that mankind created, and how a crisis can be turned into an opportunity to improve the quality of life for all.

Enough has been written and printed about climate change, or global warming, to fell a few of the large rainforests of the world. Selling the theory should no longer be necessary. Common sense tells us the dynamics of climate change are true. The only questions remaining are when and how the changes are going to take place. Common sense also tells us how to stop climate change, although human nature is such that we believe that it is someone else's responsibility. The balance between selfish desire and altruism will never be struck. The only way to prevent climate change is to turn it into a business, and that is what the world is doing right now.

Despite an overwhelming body of real scientific evidence, there is still a school of thought that believes that climate change is not a threat. And of those who do believe the evidence, there is a vocal minority that in fact welcomes the prospect of a warmer atmosphere and feels that it will ultimately be to our benefit. First of all, we should be totally frank. For any resident of northern Ontario, Iceland or upper Siberia, the prospect of global warming may be not entirely unattractive. Except for a dedicated band of winter sports enthusiasts, the majority of the world finds snow attractive only in theory, and then perhaps only once a year on a very special evening. If a model could be found whereby we could all do our part to bring about a moderate warming of the earth's atmosphere, it is likely that many of us would instantaneously unite in the effort. Imagine the prospect of growing bananas on the banks of Lake Michigan, or planting a vineyard in the highlands of Scotland. The good news is that these may be real possibilities in the very near future. Thanks to the efforts of each and every one of us, Stockholm might shortly be designated as the summer fun capital of the future. The bad news is that there are, unfortunately, a few billion reasons why the prospect of palm trees in Reykjavik should not fill us with joy, and we all know what these are. Climate change will unfortunately not manifest itself by a slow and steady warming of the atmosphere. Change will be erratic and sometimes violent, and will result in ecological disasters beyond the scope of anything we have experienced in the recent past.

Rising sea levels, the melting of the Greenland ice sheet at the rate of 12 cubic miles a year, and the increasing incidence of massive and more frequent storm formations are all compelling evidence of climate change. Just as warm air expands, so does warm water. The melting of the ice cap, coupled with water expansion, will lead to a rise in sea levels, causing coastal flooding.[1] Certain areas of the world will become wetter or dryer, and the weather will become more unpredictable and violent. The insurance industry is going to see massive damage claims in the not too distant future as the result of more violent weather. Crop yields will also change. Paradoxically, these may rise in many cases. In general, the health of all living things will deteriorate as new tropical diseases and parasites are introduced to temperate regions. Water supplies will also be affected, although, once again, some areas will show improvement.

The problem is that global warming is caused by people, all of whom have an equal right to eat, house themselves, keep themselves warm and take transport to work. By the year 2050 there will be eight billion people in the world. All of these people produce greenhouse gases to varying extents. There are a number of gases that contribute to global

[1] This is a particular problem for low-lying nations that are vulnerable to a rise in the level of the ocean. These nations tend to be small, and have little influence on international policy. In order to communicate their position more effectively, they have formed the Alliance of Small Island States (AOSIS).

warming, some of which are far more powerful than others.[2] Since carbon dioxide (CO_2) is the most prevalent, this is taken as the benchmark, and all the rest are assessed in terms of CO_2. For instance, one ton of methane is equivalent to 21 tons of CO_2.[3] Carbon levels have always varied in the atmosphere, and are the result of natural as well as man-made activities. Carbon dioxide leaks naturally from the earth's surface into the atmosphere, as well as being expelled by all living things through the simple act of breathing. Some carbon is soaked up by plants through the process of photosynthesis, although the primary "consumer" of carbon is the ocean. The oceans currently hold about 40 000 billion tons of carbon, and the atmosphere contains 745 billion tons. Burning fossil fuels at current rates creates around six billion tons of carbon, half of which is retained in the atmosphere. And this is the root of the problem. When gases such as CO_2 build up in the atmosphere, they effectively trap the heat given off by the earth, which leads to global warming.[4] The amount of carbon retained in the atmosphere is estimated to have increased by just under 30% since the start of the Industrial Revolution. The Intergovernmental Panel on Climate Change (IPCC) projects that the level will double from pre-industrial levels by the end of the twenty-first century.

[2]   The greenhouse gases, in the context of the Kyoto Protocol (Annex I), are carbon dioxide (CO_2), methane (CH_4), nitrous oxide (N_2O), hydrofluorocarbons (HFCs), perfluorocarbons (PFCs), and sulfur hexafluoride (SF_6). There are a number of other greenhouse gases, but those we have just cited are the main anthropogenic gases that we can control. Note that new greenhouse gases are still being identified.

[3]   For conversion factors, see *Global Warming Potential* in the glossary.

[4]   To be a little more precise, global warming is all about longwave radiation. In simple terms, the sun warms the earth, and this heat is emitted in the form of longwave radiation. The greenhouse gases form a barrier that stops this radiation leaving the atmosphere, and so the earth retains more heat than would otherwise be the case, just like a giant greenhouse.

If we accept that a lot is at stake, and we are prepared to spend the money to fix it, it is important that we take the right approach. Before we go any further we should draw a line in the sand between those who have helped identify the problem and focused the world's attention, and those who have the ability to solve it. In other words, to draw a line between the environmentalists and the industrialists. Do not get us wrong: we have a lot to thank the environmentalists for – they are passionate believers who are vocal enough to draw attention to an issue.[5] But in the same way as you trust your family doctor to diagnose a problem, the specialist is the one who prescribes the cure. In this case, it is now the job of the industrialists and politicians to decide whether to address the problem, and how to go about it.

Global warming is a landmark issue. Never before have we addressed a more complex problem on such a global scale. The sheer logistical problem of bringing more than 180 countries together in one forum and attempting to build a framework for the solution is almost mind-boggling. In the past decade, global warming has gone from being an issue to being a mini-industry that employs thousands of people. It has matured from a concept to a reputable theory and now into a universally accepted truth, all in a phenomenally short time. In doing so, it is now a cause on which to build careers and remodel industry. There are over 2500 scientists appointed by the United Nations (UN) to monitor and assess the extent of climate change, and work on programs to mitigate its effect. Global warming as an industry has spawned research centers, think tanks, environmental action groups, thousands of well groomed policy workers, and now even a financial market. Enough committees,

---

[5] There is a link between romanticism and the environmental movement. Graham Burgess recently addressed the Bath Philosophical Society on this issue, as well as the role of mysticism and spiritualism within the movement. 'Questioning the motives of environmentalism', the *Independent*, 4 August 2000, section 2, p. 4.

working groups and acronyms have been created to make any hardened
Pentagon bureaucrat proud.

There have been countless meetings over the past couple of decades
devoted to the problem of climate change, and during the process an
entire new lexicon has been contrived. These include IPCC, UNFCCC,
COP and Kyoto, amongst others. The semantics of global warming are
anything but interesting, but they are necessary to understanding what
the world is doing to address the problem.

Global warming became big news in the summer of 1988, when Dr
James Hansen, head of the US government's Goddard Institute of Space
Studies, addressed a Senate Committee in Washington. America was in
the grips of a severe heatwave, accompanied by drought in certain areas,
when Hansen told the assembled lawmakers that the unusually high
temperatures experienced during the decade were almost certainly the
result of a build-up in greenhouse gases in the atmosphere. Hansen had at
his fingertips perhaps more data than any other scientist in the world on
the effects of pollution in the atmosphere, which gave his statement
instant credibility. He has since carried the mantle as the unofficial Father
of Global Warming. At the end of that same year, the UN's National
Assembly approved the creation of the IPCC. Their first report, issued in
1990, confirmed Hansen's statements. Another, even longer acronym
was added to the language in 1992 at the Rio de Janeiro Earth Summit,
when 154 countries signed the United Nations Framework Convention
on Climate Change (UNFCCC). The official body authorized to debate
this agreement is the Conference of Parties (COP), which held their first
meeting in 1995, now referred to as COP-1.

The milestone came at the COP-3 meeting in Kyoto in 1997, attended
by US Vice President Al Gore, where the parties signed the Kyoto
Protocol: a framework that calls for mandatory action to reduce the
emission of greenhouse gases. As with any agreement involving thousands
of policy negotiators from 180 countries, substantial flaws exist in the

international framework that has been drawn up to address the problem of climate change.

Interestingly, former President George Bush, a moderate Republican, is the person credited with getting this process going back in 1990 and involving a then reluctant international community of nations in the process. The initiative has now been co-opted by the Democrats, and America's role in the process has concurrently been diminished by more environmentally active European nations.

One of the key outcomes from the Kyoto meetings was a decision to split the world into two blocs. A separation was made between the so-called Annex I countries[6] – the major developed countries of the world – and the non-Annex I countries – the nations of the developing world. In essence, the protocol calls for Annex I countries to make an overall reduction of 5% in greenhouse gas emissions by 2010[7] from 1990 levels.[8] Non-Annex I countries are not required to make any cuts. The logic behind this is that the developed nations are much better placed economically to make the cuts, while the developing nations cannot make the investment required to become more energy efficient, and can ill afford any additional expense that potentially slows their growth. A good deal of intelligence and imagination went into structuring the agreement, which goes far beyond simply mandating cuts across the board. As the emission of greenhouse gases into the earth's atmosphere is a global, rather than local, pollution problem, it makes no difference if the level emissions are cut in Africa or North America, so long as the total level of emissions fall. In other words, the signatories of the Kyoto Protocol accepted the logic of giving the signing countries a certain amount of leeway in achieving their targets, which can be achieved through the

[6] Called Annex I because they are listed in Annex I of the UNFCCC.
[7] It is actually the average for the period 2008–2012.
[8] While the average across the Annex I countries is 5.2%, individual nations have different target levels listed in the glossary.

introduction of three different types of Flexibility Mechanisms. The rules and the scope of these Flexibility Mechanisms are high on the agenda of the COP-6 meeting in the Hague in November 2000.

The most controversial of the mechanisms is the creation of a financial market to trade in pollution credits. At the instigation of the Americans, the UN agreed that nations that effectively cut their emissions below target levels could trade their surplus credits to other nations that were less successful. Accordingly, each nation can then allow trading either domestically or internationally for industries that are required to meet internal emission targets. Under this system, an aluminum smelter based in the UK, which is required to reduce emissions by a certain degree, is given a choice: it can invest in new clean technology or buy credits from other companies that have exceeded their target levels. What sounds like an evil trade on the surface is in fact a brilliant way of limiting the economic impact of change. It also enables governments to pass the hard decisions back to the private sector, and hence wash their hands of any adverse consequences. The trading of pollution credits is of nominal interest, but the attachment of a theoretical value to clean air is of great importance to the financial markets. If clean air has a monetary value, particularly over a period of time, then that value can be applied to the installation of technology that eradicates greenhouse gas emissions. Quite simply, an industry can finance a major project to clean the air by issuing a bond in the capital markets, and use the revenue stream derived from the sale of emission credits to pay off the debt.

Until now, pumping noxious emissions in the air has been free, just as our forebears thought nothing of dumping sewage in rivers and lakes, or mining land or chopping down native forests. Nature has historically been viewed as a resource open to exploitation by all. This view changed dramatically in the last century, as civilized nations made considerable efforts to clean up pollution in lakes, rivers and oceans. Now, mankind has taken a step further and is levying a charge against itself for polluting the atmosphere, which in turn will create a value for cutting down on levels of emissions.

Trading emission credits is the easiest of the Flexibility Mechanisms to put in place. Although few countries have yet to set up such a market, it is expected that the European Union (EU) will shortly allow trading between companies. The two other Flexibility Mechanisms are far more difficult to enact, as they involve international collaboration and a bureaucracy in place to attest to the validity of each transaction. Both of these mechanisms are project based, and are designed to encourage long-term investment in ventures that reduce emissions. The payoff for the investor is that the emission reductions they create can either be used to help them meet their own targets or be sold in the new pollution credits market. The Annex I/non-Annex I split is the delineation that is used to distinguish the two project-based Flexibility Mechanisms. Clean Development Mechanisms (CDMs) provide Annex I countries credits for clean air projects in the developing world. Joint Implementation Mechanisms provide credits for Annex I countries by undertaking the same type of projects in other developed countries. The guidelines for validating these types of mechanisms have yet to be determined fully. They are both designed to lessen the cost of change and to encourage investment in the developing world. The most important development to come out of Kyoto, however, was the provision allowing the trading of "carbon credits" among Annex I countries.

The important dates for the Kyoto Protocol are 1990 (the "base" year) and 2010 (the "first commitment period"). Between these dates, the world's population is expected to grow from 5.3 billion to 6.8 billion, with most of that increase in the non-Annex I countries. Our conservative estimates suggest that even if Annex I countries decrease their emissions by 5%,[9] and non-Annex I countries emissions per head are

9   Assuming they do not take advantage of CDM projects, which address emission problems in developing countries.

unchanged, actual total emissions will still be 10% higher in 2010 than they were in 1990. This is all down to population growth in a part of the world that is outside the reach of the Kyoto Protocol.

While the formula proposed in the Kyoto Protocol quite rightly calls upon the top 20% of the population to cut their emissions of CO_2 by varying degrees, the problem, as the Americans keep pointing out, is that the agreement in its current form is flawed. An important dimension of the problem, and one that often appears to be overlooked, is that there are simply too many people in the world, and there are more on the way. The world's population growth has slowed to some extent in the past decade, but it is still increasing at the rate of 80 million a year. It is somewhat fortuitous that the real population explosion is occurring in the developing world, which accounts for less than 40% of the world's energy consumption. Currently, 1.6 billion people of the world's total population of six billion do not have access to commercial energy. A further 3.2 billion people in the world do not enjoy regular, uninterrupted supplies of energy. The majority of energy consumption is taken up by the lucky 1.2 billion people who live in industrialized countries. The fortunate 20% of the global population of the world consume, on average, five tons of energy per capita per year, whereas the lowliest 32% of the population consume just 0.2 tons of energy per capita per year, most of this being biomass, or "carbon neutral" fuel.

With the exception of the poorest of the earth's population, who have the least resources and are carbon efficient only by default, the rest of mankind seems hell-bent on generating as much CO_2 as is humanly possible. This is as true for the very rich countries as it is for the countries on the cusp of development. Countries with rapidly growing populations may be forgiven for increasing their emissions, but those countries with relatively stable populations, such as the USA, Japan and Germany, are increasing their emissions by even greater rates.

Motivating the world to make the sort of investment necessary to significantly alter the equation of global warming means staking out what is politically feasible and what is not. There is a realpolitick to environmental change. People will welcome change that improves their lives. The thought of Americans relinquishing their sport utility vehicles in preference for bicycles is an idea close to the heart of every environmentalist, but it is about as far away from being practically feasible as the possibility of sticking a windmill in everyone's back yard. The methane produced by herds of cattle, sheep and other grazing animals is also another problem that is outside the realm of environmental action. The world is not about to embrace vegetarianism on a wholesale basis, nor are farmers about to significantly alter the way they produce food. In Ireland, a recently commissioned study on greenhouse gases concluded that the only significant reduction possible on a national scale would be to end all animal husbandry throughout the Republic. Not only would greenhouse gas production be cut significantly, but the country would have access to cheaper food and the economy would benefit significantly by ending subsidies to farmers. The only problem with this formula is that Ireland is still primarily an agrarian society, and the farmers constitute the biggest voting block in the country.

In the developing world, governments are not about to restrict the rights of farmers to cut down virgin rainforests in order to clear land for the planting of crops. Instead of simple lifestyle decisions, these are survival decisions. The realpolitick of environmental change is all about targeting winnable battles. Winnable battles will be fought first in North America, the EU and Japan.

The solutions to global warming should be practical and real, and, most importantly, should not bankrupt us. If false solutions are imposed on the taxpayers of the Annex I countries, and these prove too expensive to bear, the battle against global warming will swiftly move into the ballot box and will be lost instantaneously. Global warming is more of a political than a scientific battle. This book will demonstrate how the problem can be solved without pushing industry offshore, or taxing the citizens of the developed world into penury. We will discuss all the solutions, identify those that work, and demonstrate how money can be pushed in the right directions. There will be changes in industry, and a new model for pricing energy and power, but there will also be new growth areas for the economy, and a better lifestyle for all. But there is no point in the taxpayers of the developed world cleaning up their own environment if the hole is being filled by growing pollution in the developing world. We cannot simply push the problem to another part of the globe, either by making the dirtiest fuels cheaper or making it easier for polluting industries to build new factories in developing world cities. At the same time that we want to demonstrate that solving this problem will enrich the lives of those in the developed world, we will show how an intelligent strategy will raise the standard of living of the poorest people on earth. They have the most to lose in this equation, but we all have a lot to gain.

If we remember that it has taken the world 150 years to create this problem, we can understand that it is not going to be sorted out overnight. The fact is that the solution to global warming is within our grasp right now, and that solution involves a massive investment in public transport, infrastructure and new technologies. The real costs of change, which will be borne mainly by the developed world, may initially run in excess of $500 billion a year. The solutions to global warming are very simple, but some are very costly to enact. They include reducing or negating the use of carbon-based fuels to generate electrical power, streamlining manufacturing processes, promoting recycling of certain materials and, most importantly, limiting the use of the internal combustion engine. The world also has to unite to clean up the oceans in an effort to make sure that this important carbon sink continues to function well into the future.

Nobody likes to bandy about the figure of $500 billion a year. It is probably a realistic figure, but it should not be thought of as a cost. If it were a cost, it would be politically unacceptable. This is the price of the new investment required to resolve this problem, which will be channelled into new industries and municipal projects that will create jobs and spur economic growth. It is the price for changing the way industry makes products and utilities generate power. It is the cost of changing the way people get to work, or heat their homes in the dead of winter. It is a cost that will provide an economic and environmental return, and it is also a cost that will go away at a certain point. This problem needs only money and intelligence to fix it, and the solution will come much sooner than expected. As such, it is an investment in the future, not a cost.

There has been a degree of research put into "pricing" the cost of pollution in the future, the purpose of which is to attempt to render industry with a value for clean air in the coming years and provide an incentive for instituting change now. The validity of this data is open to challenge, as the research has been done using theoretical models that do not account for technological leaps that may lessen the cost of change or for dramatic changes in the economic performance of certain countries. Certain sectors of the media have latched on to this information and have tried to estimate the cost of complying with the Kyoto Protocol using these projections and price data from the nascent pollution trading market.[10] If this approach were taken, then the value of reducing CO_2 emissions to Kyoto Protocol target levels could be calculated as something in the range of $5 billion.[11] This is of a different order of magnitude to the estimated costs of real change to the way we live. The IPCC quotes various figures, which range from a cost of $240 billion to a net benefit of

[10] This market does not yet really exist, although one or two trades have taken place, but there is obviously a lot of speculation.

[11] Based on Annex 1 volume of 10 billion tons of CO_2 emitted per year, reduced by 5% at a price of $10/ton.

$60 billion.[12] To put this number in context, it took about $5 billion to build an extension on to one London Underground line, which may result in 13 000 fewer vehicle journeys a day in London. It is fairly evident that $5 billion is merely a drop in the bucket of the total cost of global change. We will demonstrate that the real "costs" of change are minimal, but that the investment required to live in a carbon-free world will be considerable. We are not going to resolve this problem by pricing electricity out of the reach of the middle classes, or by turning gasoline into a luxury good. The capital markets can be mobilized to "invest" our way out of this problem. The cost of investment might be high, but it may mean that the cost of driving our cars or turning on the lights might in fact be cheaper in the future.

Given the importance of trading as part of the solution, it is worth a quick diversion to look at trading in its own right. Traders do not work in a vacuum; there has to be a physical business upon which to base the trading. For the trading of emission credits to become a viable business, a ton of CO_2 must have a price based upon genuine supply and demand. Legislation will restrict the supply of available credits for which the power companies have to compete. At this point, a power company has to decide on whether it buys credits and continues to pollute, or whether it invests in cleaner technology. It is this financial decision on which trading can be built, and until this is a decision that power companies *have* to make, a trading market cannot exist. The role of trading is to increase the number of choices the power companies have, and so provide additional flexibility and reduce the cost of change. The bottom line is that trading is just the "oil" that makes real change happen more easily, but it does not actually cut emissions. Although it might cost $500 billion a year to make real change, the actual trading market in CO_2 emissions might have a turnover of just $5 billion, or 1% of the total amount.

[12] The net benefit to the OECD economies would arise from increased efficiencies and a decrease in the consumption of energy.

The theory that the world can solely use carbon credits to trade itself out of impending disaster ignores the fact that the majority of greenhouse gases are not produced by industry but are, in fact, the result of the lifestyles we lead. They will not go away without a government commitment to infrastructure development on a local and national level. Emissions from industry can be valued only if a fair global market is created, and this also involves a government commitment. The one factor in favor of creating a global market to trade credits is that the problem of greenhouse gases is not local. Simply because it makes no difference whether CO_2 is emitted from Nairobi or Seattle, price differentials will arise, which will push capital to the least costly areas of the world. But without stringent control, there will be no guarantees that genuine changes will occur.

Environmental finance will grow to be one of the biggest businesses in the world, but it will not be based to any great extent on the trading of emissions. Emissions trading may provide a short-term pricing structure for short-term needs, but the real business of environmental finance will be about financing major industry and government-led projects. It will also involve changing the entire investment formula for venture capital, corporate finance and long-term investment strategy.

Enacting real change is not a cost, but a necessary investment. It is not money that goes down a dark hole; it employs countless thousands of people, creates new industries, spurs economic growth and makes the world a better place to live in. Not only will the benefits extend to the developed world, but a plan of real action will free up cleaner carbon-based fuels for the developing world, which will improve the quality of life for all.

Few of us think that pollution is a good thing. On a micro basis, humans have the ability to band together and act quickly to improve the quality of life. Less than half a century ago, killer fogs used to engulf London, killing hundreds of inhabitants at a time. The simple banning of individual coal fires instantly eliminated the problem and improved the quality of life for all. In Los Angeles, where the air is something people can taste, a clean air initiative has been launched that is making a significant dent in the pollution problem. Few of us would take a trip to the environmental wasteland that used to be the Aral Sea and marvel at the great accomplishments of the Soviet state. The vast majority of the world's population would much prefer to breathe clean air, drink clean water and bathe in pristine oceans. Whether or not we embrace the environmentalists' most dire predictions, the majority of the world's population recognizes there are problems with the environment and would choose to act upon these issues in a positive manner rather than ignore the problem and hope it goes away. Just as most of us support environmental action, the majority of the population is also intelligent enough to recognize what is real action and what is in fact a whitewash. Cleaning the oceans, lakes and rivers, as well as the atmosphere, takes time, effort and, more importantly, real money. The challenge the world faces right now is to think globally, not locally. This mindset may take a while to sink in.

Despite the discord surrounding the agreement, the world should be applauded for getting together and addressing the problem. Whatever environmentalists may think of industry leaders, many of the top executives of the world are united in their concern over this problem. Even if this concern is fostered only by an effort to create a "green" image, most of the developed world's major corporations are making some effort to reduce their greenhouse gas emissions. The world's energy and power companies are taking a longer-term view. They know that they will *have* to address this problem sooner or later, and it will be cheaper to start seeking a solution now.

The January 2000 meeting of the World Economic Forum in Davos, Switzerland addressed all the major social and ecological problems facing mankind, and concluded that global warming was the most important issue. The conference designated climate change as the world's most pressing problem, and also voted it as the issue where business could most effectively adopt a leadership role.

For business leaders to embrace the problem is significant, not because they care more about the environment than the average person, but because they are intelligent enough to sense a possible mood swing among the people of the world. Global warming has been an issue in the back of people's minds for some time, but within this decade it will move to the forefront of our thoughts. When this occurs, governments and industries will respond. The smartest business leaders and politicians are positioning themselves for this time in order to ensure that they are one step ahead of popular sentiment.

2

AMERICA STRIKES OUT

It is theoretically possible to score a "run" in the American game of baseball by striking out. This would not be an "earned run", but would count in the score nonetheless. Under the rules of the game, the lucky player would have to benefit from at least one further "error" to score. Although it is a highly unlikely event, and would make the opposing baseball team the laughing stock of the stadium, more Americans know the arcane rules that govern baseball than know what percentage vote is required for the US Senate to ratify a foreign treaty.[1] Baseball is enjoyable only if the spectator understands the hundreds of rules that govern the way the game is played and scored, and this virtually requires growing up in America.[2] Most Europeans who are dragged along to their first Yankees or Red Sox game by overenthusiastic American friends find the event about as interesting as watching paint dry. The American political system is also governed by hundreds of even more arcane rules, and understanding how a concept turns into a proposed bill, and eventually into law, requires an immersion into the subject virtually from birth. The American

---

[1] Ratification of a foreign treaty requires a two-thirds majority vote in the US Senate.

[2] Or Puerto Rico, Venezuela, Mexico, Japan, the Dominican Republic, even Australia, but, most importantly, Cuba.

political system may seem mystifying to most Europeans,[3] although to most Americans the Parliamentary system of government seems like a dictatorship by the majority.

A long discourse on the inner workings of the American legislative system, and the process that Congress would have to undertake to ratify the Kyoto Protocol, would be about as fascinating to any European as a seven-day cricket match would be to any red-blooded American. Fortunately, it is unnecessary, because America is not about to ratify the Kyoto Protocol now, or at any time in the near future. The possibility is not realistic, even if snow became a distant memory in Alaska and the state of Florida became an underwater theme park. This is not to say that Americans are bad, or hell-bent on doing their level best to end life as we know it. Americans do care tremendously about the environment, and most would support any effort to reduce the possibility of climate change. America instigated the entire international effort that led to the formulation of the Kyoto Protocol. Although the majority of Americans would support an international effort to reduce greenhouse gas emissions, they are simply not about to put themselves on the same level playing field as the rest of the world. Americans will not allow themselves to be governed by the same rules as Ecuadorians, Vietnamese or Ukrainians, nor will they allow their lifestyles to come under the scrutiny of a critical world. This is equally true for the most rabidly conservative tobacco farmer from South Carolina as it is for the most politically liberal and environmentally concerned housewife in Marin County.

Interestingly enough, it is not necessary for America to formally ratify the Kyoto Protocol for it to comply with the agreement.[4] There have

[3]   Where else in the world can a government be effectively "shut down" for almost a year because of a private sexual act between two adults?

[4]   America did sign and ratify the UNFCCC under which the Kyoto Protocol was drafted. To put the protocol into force requires the ratification of 55 countries, accounting for at least 55% of the 1990 emissions of Annex I countries. America accounts for 40% of the total amount of greenhouse gas emissions.

been five major environmental treaties in the past two decades, none of which America ratified, although the USA has complied with the terms of all the treaties. This is what is happening now, and probably will be the policy of US administrations in the future. The executive branch of government in America has some freedom to be openly disingenuous, and it has a history of doing this when it comes to politically unpopular international agreements. However, by adopting this route, the level of compliance will never be complete and the tendency to look at ways of creatively circumventing domestic compliance will be taken to an art form.

The Clinton administration has done about as much as is legally possible to lay the groundwork for compliance with the Kyoto Protocol, without violating the requirement to provide for Congressional "advice and consent" on international treaties. The administration is effectively holding the Kyoto Protocol in suspense until the balance of power changes in the upper house, which is unlikely to occur until at least the 108th Congress convenes in 2003. US Senators serve terms of six years, and as only one-third are up for re-election every two years, even a landslide victory by either the Republicans or Democrats in the next election would do little to change the balance of power in the Senate.

Compliance with the Kyoto Protocol has been undertaken by the Environmental Protection Agency (EPA) and the Department of Energy (DOE). Scientific assessment is conducted by the US Global Climate Change Research Program (USGCCRP), which was set up in 1990 under the Bush administration. The strategy the executive branch has used to date has been to attempt to classify greenhouse gases as pollutants, and thereby put them under the control of the Clean Air Act. By doing this, the federal government can force states to reduce emissions. Classifying CO_2 as a suddenly discovered new pollutant, and funding the reduction of emissions, has proved more difficult than imagined. The Republican Congressional opposition has been fighting this effort. One Republican

Congressman, Joe Knollenberg from Michigan, has successfully attached a provision to various appropriation bills for the DOE and EPA, which states, "None of the funds appropriated by this Act shall be used to propose or issue rules, regulations, decrees, or orders for the purpose of implementation, or in preparation for implementation, of the Kyoto Protocol."[5] In 1998, Republican Senator John Ashcroft proposed a major bill, the Economic Growth and Sovereignty Protection Act, designed specifically to shut down all government attempts to comply with the Kyoto Protocol. The bill was lost in committee hearings.[6]

Conservative think tanks in the USA have united in their opposition to the Kyoto Protocol under the banner of the Cooler Heads Coalition. This group includes about 20 various partisan and nonpartisan organizations, led by the Competitive Enterprise Institute (CEI), a libertarian think tank with links to neither the Democrats nor the Republicans.[7] The CEI has been effective in limiting back-door implementation of the Kyoto Protocol by the executive branch of the government. The Cooler Heads Coalition filed suit against the EPA in March 2000, demanding documents from the EPA that would reveal circumspect government efforts to bring about de facto compliance with the Kyoto Protocol. They have specifically targeted EPA administrator, Carol Browner, as the leader of the administration's effort. Browner is a former legislative assistant to Al Gore. A leaked memo written by Browner purportedly describes in detail methods of interpreting the Clean Air Act in a manner that would classify CO_2 as a pollutant. Known as the Climate Change Action Plan, the memo recommended the implementation of a "greenhouse gas tax" that would result in a 50 cent charge on every gallon of gasoline sold in the USA.

Although a number of Americans would classify themselves as polit-

[5]   The Knollenberg restrictions are vague in their wording and open to interpretation.

[6]   Bill S2019 stalled in the Environment and Public Works Committee.

[7]   The Libertarian Party is opposed to almost all government intervention in the personal and business affairs of citizens.

ically conservative, this does not mean they are anti-environmentalists. In a recent poll conducted by the Gallup Organization,[8] some 83% of Americans agreed with the goals of the environmental movement, and 68% thought the government was doing too little to protect the environment. But when asked how they ranked environmental concern in relation to other issues, Americans ranked it less important than education, healthcare, crime and "family values". In fact, it was placed eighth on a list of 12 issues, just behind gun control. Global warming was specifically considered an important issue by 40% of the voters. In terms of all potential environmental issues, Americans were most concerned with nuclear waste, toxic waste, water pollution and the loss of tropical rainforests. Also of concern were the depletion of the ozone layer and local air pollution.

It takes a relative level of sophistication for the average voter to differentiate between all atmospheric pollution issues, including local air pollution, depletion of the ozone layer, acid rain and the build-up of greenhouse gases. All are interlinked to some extent, with the exception of the depletion of the ozone layer, which is a simple problem with a simple solution. The other problems – local air pollution, acid rain and global warming – are all caused by the burning of fossil fuels.

Ozone forms a protective layer in the upper atmosphere, screening out harmful ultraviolet rays. Chlorofluorocarbons (CFCs) are responsible for destroying the ozone layer. The Montreal Protocol effectively banned the use of CFCs after the year 2000. Unfortunately, CFCs have been replaced by HFCs and PFCs, which are now known to be powerful greenhouse gases.

Acid rain is the result of high levels of sulfur dioxide (SO_2) and nitrous oxide (NO_2) in the lower atmosphere generated by the burning of coal in the industrial Midwest. Acid rain destroys forests and acidifies lakes and

---

[8]   Lydia Saad and Riley E. Dunlap, *Americans are Environmentally Friendly, but Issue not Seen as Urgent Problem*, Gallup News Service, 17 April 2000. Poll conducted 3–9 April 2000.

rivers in northeast USA and Canada. In a uniquely American way, the government decided to resolve the problem of acid rain by creating a market in pollution. This market is the precursor to what is imagined the global market in greenhouse gas emission credits will be, except on an international scale. Unfortunately, the creation of the SO_2 and NO_2 (SOx and NOx) market has failed to create an asset class[9] in pollution credits, which was the original intention of the architects of the system. Without the creation of a new asset class, the polluters are unable to securitize debt[10] in the capital markets to finance the installation of scrubbers, or for wholesale conversion to cleaner burning fuels. The market is delivering cleaner air, but is not totally eliminating the problem of acid rain. Like everything else, the problem comes down to size. The number of participants, the size of the credits and the value of the credits are just not large enough to create the critical mass that is required for a vibrant and transparent market. Another problem is that environmentalists themselves are preventing the market from resolving the problem. By pushing through legislation that fines the utilities an amount that is equal to the profits they make by selling emission permits, they have single-handedly taken all the incentives out of the market. In New York State, environmental pressure groups have barred all utilities from participating in the market. Another more nebulous factor that has hindered progress is the failure to attract the interest of investment bankers, who would be capable of shaping legislation in order to create a market that works.

Local air pollution, like that experienced in Los Angeles, is primarily the result of car exhaust fumes. The smog that covers southern California is high in particulates, which cause lung cancers and raise levels of asthma in children and the elderly. Particulates hover in the lower atmosphere and eventually fall to earth. Although local air pollution is a contributor

[9] By "asset class" we mean something in which people or companies can invest, in the same way as they do in the stock and bond markets.

[10] Securitizing debt means guaranteeing by using a set of future cash flows. In this case, the cash flow would derive from the value of the emission credits.

to global warming, the problem of smog is localized and will harm those only downwind from the area.

Americans are concerned about all types of atmospheric pollution, and it has only been the media's inability to convey the urgency of the climate change issue that has prevented it from becoming a major concern of the American people. The problem is that a popular concern for environmental causes does not translate immediately into political concern. Unlike in the 1960s and 1970s, when the political establishment was more liberal than the voters and therefore was able to push through unpopular legislation dealing with race relations and economic injustices, the political establishment now in America is more conservative than the voters. Neither of the two main political parties has made the environment a priority. The Democratic Party is, at best, lukewarm about "green" issues, while the Republican Party is vehemently opposed to virtually all environmental causes.

In any other country in the world, the political left would typically be the primary instigator of any environmentally sensitive legislation. The problem in America is that the political left wing, or liberal establishment, has been inexplicably phased out of existence. Although it is difficult for most Americans to have the perspective to understand this, the country now has only two political ideologies: conservative and, for want of a better description, radically conservative. There are two national print media outlets for the opposing political parties: the *New York Times* represents the Democrats and the *Wall Street Journal* is the voice for the Republicans. Despite the perceptions of its own editorial staff, the *New York Times* is, at least by international standards, politically conservative in its views, and the *Wall Street Journal*[11] is so radically right

---

[11] To further infuriate the scattered remains of the liberal establishment in America, the views of the *Wall Street Journal* may be politically contentious, but many consider it to be a more concise and better written newspaper than the *New York Times*.

wing that its editorial stance on a number of issues, including the environment, is nothing less than interesting. In America, the views of these respective newspapers have an enormous influence on the political establishment, perhaps greater in power than the electorate. To put this into perspective, and in the context of the issue of global warming, only in America would a newspaper that effectively represented the mainstream views of a major political party unabashedly print an article entitled "The rainforest doesn't need saving".[12] Part of the scientific justification that the author of the article cited to back up his claim that deforestation of tropical rainforests was a liberal myth were the observations of an old woman in an African village who claimed that "there are now too many trees"!

In this sort of political environment, where the Republican Party can publicly claim that "the earth is balanced, Al Gore is not", it is difficult to imagine that any significant environmental initiatives will come out of the next session of Congress. A fringe US political group, the Reform Party, which is actually an offshoot of the Republican Party, openly opposes the ratification of the Kyoto Protocol. The stated position of the Republican Party is that the treaty has to be renegotiated to bring in the developing world. The Democratic Party is in favor of ratifying the treaty, although the chances of bringing this about are almost nil, given the lock hold the opposition has on Congress. Assuming the political status quo continues on into the next administration, even de facto compliance will prove difficult when expenditures have to be pushed through in the new budget. Any "hot air" trade with Russia will require real cash, and opposition will be tough when the new budget is debated.

The American electorate has not exactly spent the last decade clamoring for environmental action. Membership in environmental action groups, such as Greenpeace, has fallen significantly, and with no national

[12] Philip Stott, 'The rainforest doesn't need saving', *Wall Street Journal*, 10 July 2000.

liberal press to act as a forum for debate, the issue has gradually disappeared from the public consciousness. On top of this, the nation has enjoyed a steady and robust economic expansion that has bred an unparalleled level of political complacency that has played into the hands of conservative interests. Actual voting patterns in the USA bear little relation to public sentiment. Until "events" occur that rock the confidence of the electorate, it is unlikely that the USA will be motivated to take the mantle of environmental leadership. This is not to say that each and every American is not indirectly doing their dead level best to bring about these "events".

During the last 10 years, subsequent to the US ratification of the Framework Convention on Climate Change, the nation has responded by increasing the emissions of greenhouse gases at an astounding rate. Bearing in mind that the USA is meant to cut emissions of greenhouse gases from 1990 levels, even minimal compliance will prove next to impossible given the rapid rate of growth the USA has sustained, and the profligate use of fossil fuels the country has relied upon to sustain this growth. During the past decade, CO_2 emissions in the USA grew by 12%. Growth in emissions from the transportation sector was highest, although residential, commercial and industrial sectors were not far behind. During 1999 the amount of total emissions grew by 1% alone, and growth might be even higher in the year 2000. What is most astounding about these figures is the type of fuel America is relying upon to sustain its growth. While the rest of the developed world has made a significant effort to reduce the burning of coal, America has increased consumption by almost 13% in the past decade, and this has been primarily for the generation of electrical power. The consumption of cleaner burning natural gas has also increased, but the USA is still burning coal to produce power, which, given the low cost of the conversion to natural gas, is irrational. During this period, "heating degree days", or days that were cold enough to warrant a significant increase in home and office heating requirements, were over 6% lower than in the previous period. Conversely, "cooling degree days" were up by over 3%. Nuclear and hydroelectric power generation increased significantly to offset demand. Hydroelectric generation capacity was increased due to higher levels of precipitation.[13]

There is an interested party out in the world that has the ability to save America from being branded as an environmental outlaw, although the terms of the "deal" on offer do nothing less than undermine the entire intent of the global effort to limit greenhouse gas emissions. The unlikely savior of the USA is none other than its old arch-enemy, Russia. Under the terms of the Kyoto Protocol, Russia is required only to sustain emissions at 1990 levels. Given the collapse of the industrial sector, emissions are now less than 70% of the target figure, giving Russia an "emission credit" of a few billion tons of CO_2. All the USA has to do is negotiate a fair price for these credits with Russia, and use them to meet its own targets. The ethics of the transaction are dubious, but by striking a deal with Russia, America can still meet minimal compliance standards. Needless to say, the rest of the developed world, which is actually taking the problem somewhat seriously, is less than enthusiastic about the transaction. It is unlikely that Russia would find an alternative buyer for its credits. America is the only potential purchaser on the market, giving it increased leverage in price negotiations.

If America were to take a different route and actually get down to the business of reducing emissions, an entirely different cost paradigm would enter into the equation. Given the current level of political resistance to compliance, if the US government presented a real program for change that came with a realistic multibillion dollar yearly cost attached, the conservative press in America would have a heyday. Real change would involve a colossal investment in public transportation, high-speed rail

[13] *US Carbon Dioxide Emissions from Energy Sources, 1999 Flash Estimate.* Energy Information Administration, US Department of Energy, June 2000.

networks, wholesale conversion from coal to gas, hydroelectric power and nuclear energy. The costs, when viewed from a short-term conservative perspective, would be unsustainable. When viewed from a longer-term investment perspective, an intense industry- and government-led effort to reduce emissions would result in new technologies and industries, and would become another area in which America could lead the world. An entirely new export market would arise for American technology, jobs would be created, and economic growth would be sustained.

Another cheaper alternative America could take would be to invest in projects in the developing world that would have the same effect on reducing greenhouse gas emissions. Building a mass transport system in a developing country is substantially cheaper than doing the same in an American city. In the case of Los Angeles, bringing about any substantial reduction in emissions is probably a hopeless cause, unless by some miracle fuel cell technology was improved and the internal combustion engine could be replaced en masse. Common sense tells us that the sprawling layout and low population density of Los Angeles defies any logical attempt to build a workable mass transit system. Nevertheless, the city has embarked upon an absurd attempt to build a subway system to nowhere, at the cost of billions of taxpayer dollars. If the city were to be held responsible for its own emission targets, and would eventually be forced to buy credits on the open market to make up for shortfalls, the most logical decision the city could make would be to stop trying to build its own mass transit capability. The wisest use of taxpayer money would be to invest the money in a mass transit project in Mexico, thereby earning credits at a much cheaper cost. This would cost the taxpayers money, and would not improve the life of the citizens of Los Angeles – a political reality that would be difficult to overcome.

One thing the Republican Party has right in America is that environmentalists should not be given the power to set policy. Americans have a right to put their own self-interests above the interests of the environmental lobby, but if a policy that works is going to be formulated, compromises will have to be made at both ends. Immediate compliance with the Kyoto Protocol is still within the grasp, even without buying "hot air" from the Russians, but it will involve some allocation of government funds to projects in the developing world as well as immediate changes in the way America uses fuel.

The complete elimination of coal use in power generation is a fairly simple matter to address. Not only would it not lead to an increase in the price of electricity, it would immediately improve the quality of the air. It would, simultaneously, significantly reduce the level of greenhouse gas emissions in the USA. Another, more politically contentious alternative is to begin a reinvestment in America's nuclear energy capabilities, bringing a number of cheaper and safer plants online. America, on average, is far less reliant on clean nuclear energy than the rest of the world. America can also choose to invest in more hydroelectric projects, although these raise as many environmental concerns as does nuclear power. The hard facts require that some politically and environmentally unpalatable choices will have to be made, and for America to maintain its levels of energy consumption, nuclear, hydroelectric and natural gas projects should be the only three choices available for the generation of electrical power.

Another overwhelming factor that America has in its favor, which has yet to be mobilized for this effort, is the tremendous power of its financial markets. If the USA actively shapes the market for the global trading of greenhouse gas emissions, and assures that it does not fall to the same fate as the domestic NOx and SOx market, American financial institutions will lead the effort for global change. If emission credits can become a new asset class, and the origination of credits can be used to securitize debt, US investment banks will create a whole new range of financial products linked to environmental finance. America will not be able to lead this effort if its government does not take an active role in the process, which means at least a de facto compliance with the Kyoto

Protocol. The venture capitalists of America will also recognize the importance of new technologies that have the potential to reduce emissions, and will change their investment models to take these into account.

Both the Democratic and Republican Parties are united in the belief that taxing the problem will not make it go away. If taxation is used as a means to shape personal and commercial energy usage, it will not only hurt those most vulnerable, but will act as a brake on economic growth. If America uses its influence on a global scale, and convinces other countries to avoid taxing the problem out of existence, capitalism can be mobilized on a massive scale to address the problem. If this is the solution the world chooses to take, the money to make the changes will come from Wall Street, not Washington.

There is a contentious debate in America about global warming, ratification of the Kyoto Protocol, and conflicts between the administration and congress regarding back-door implementations of the accord. Many of the views expressed by the conservative right wing are bound to raise the blood pressure of those who care deeply about the subject. That being said, America is at least debating the subject in the public domain. The CEI, the Cooler Heads Coalition and the platform provided by the *Wall Street Journal* offer a valuable counterpoint to the liberal press that accepts all too easily the most dire predictions provided by the environmental lobby. The requirement for "advice and consent" from the US Senate assures that no international treaty is ratified without being thoroughly examined, picked apart and analyzed for the impacts it will have on the country. American Congressmen have a responsibility first to the state or district they represent, and secondly to their political parties. They will judge the impact of ratification against the best interests of their constituents. To a European politician, American government may seem like an unadulterated mess, but when a law is passed or a treaty ratified by the US Congress, it is done with popular support, not behind closed doors and without the participation of the public.

3

THE REST OF THE WORLD

By all rights, Americans should speak French. Not only would this notion warm the heart of every Francophile in the world, but it would be a symbolic gesture that would go a long way towards paying off the debt the USA rightly owes the French. Although every American knows the story of the long winter George Washington and his ragged band of revolutionaries suffered at Valley Forge, it is not common knowledge that the War of Independence was really won by the French. Without French intervention, the British would have been able to concentrate their armies and quickly wipe out American resistance in the northern colonies. French intervention pinned down British land and naval forces and allowed the Americans to gain the upper hand in the struggle. At the Battle of Yorktown, which was the deciding engagement of the war, French troops greatly outnumbered their American counterparts. The treaty that finally provided formal recognition of American independence was signed in Paris. Not only did the French fight and die for the American cause, but the effort virtually bankrupted the country. A few years later, revolution and anarchy swept through France, probably as a direct result of the financial cost of fighting the battle for American freedom. Some of this cost was eventually recovered by selling the US

government a vast swath of the American continent at a bargain base-
ment price. Such is the cost of idealism.

The French are about to get nailed again, and not because they have
changed their ways and become bad global citizens. Quite the opposite in
fact. During the past 20 years, the French have done more to reduce
greenhouse gas emissions than virtually any other country in the world.
Although the average French person enjoys a standard of living that is
arguably better in many respects than the average American's, the
amount of greenhouse gas emissions per capita in France is less than one-
third of that in the USA. The reason the French are so clean in comparison to their former allies across the Atlantic is that they have made a
massive investment in the last 20 years in nuclear energy and public
transportation. The investment in the nuclear sector has been over one
trillion francs ($150 billion). France now generates 80% of its electricity
from nuclear power. They also have the best high-speed train system in
the world. When Americans talk about the quality of their lives, they
should compare the prospect of sitting in their sports utility vehicles
(SUVs) in endless traffic jams with the alternative of sipping a glass of
Bordeaux while watching the countryside flow by at a speed of 160 mph.

Now that reduction targets are in place, every Annex I country is
looking at the cheapest ways to implement change. For the USA,
breaking the "coal habit" will go a long way towards reducing emissions
to the first target level. This will be equally true for many eastern
European countries, and even some member states of the EU. Such
cheap change is not an alternative for the French. Even before targets
were set at 1990 levels, the French had made drastic changes in the way
they produced electricity. They will now be penalized for making
changes too soon. At the same time that they should be looking at the
cheap alternatives of buying the credits from eastern Europe or Russia,
the French are a little too idealistic to make such compromises. Although
this idealism will likely vanish when the second round of cuts is

announced, for now the French are not willing to buy credits that do not represent real reductions.

The French are set on wringing as many domestic reductions as possible out of their own industrial sector. Unfortunately, they are choosing to use tax as the weapon of change. In January 2000, the French government announced a 10-year plan addressing climate change, which calls for an initial tax of $23–$31/ton of carbon emitted into the atmosphere. This tax is expected to rise to over $76/ton by the year 2010. The plan does exempt some energy-intensive businesses to allow for voluntary reductions, but the impact of arbitrary taxation will hit most businesses very hard.

Ross Perot famously declared that the US ratification of the Nafta agreement would create a "giant sucking noise" as American factories took advantage of cheaper labor south of the border and moved their factories to Mexico. Any change in the ground rules always affects the way people play the game. The fact of the matter is that the Nafta agreement did push some factories across the Rio Grande. These industrial facilities took advantage not only of cheaper Mexican labor, but also of far less stringent environmental controls.

The French government is now imposing a new tax on its own industrial sector that will not allow companies to use the capital markets in the same way as their American counterparts to buy themselves out of the problem. It is not unsurprising to see announcements such as Lefarge's ambitious plan to take over cement production plants in India.[1] Lefarge is a big French building materials group, which produces, among other things, vast quantities of cement. Cement is one of those industries that emits huge amounts of greenhouse gases. The problem is the world has no replacement for cement, so until new technology is developed, it is a simple fact of life that the industry will continue to be environ-

---

[1] John Elliot, 'The rush to invest in Indian cement hits speed bumps', *International Herald Tribune*, 3 August 2000, p. 16.

mentally unfriendly. By diversifying its cement production into India, Lefarge is hedging itself against future environmental taxes. By imposing taxes that penalize its industry unfairly in comparison to the rest of the Annex I countries, the French are in danger of also hearing the same "sucking noises" the Americans feared when they signed the Nafta agreement.

For a global market to be created and function well, every industrial company in the Annex I countries should be allowed to operate under the same rules. France is doing nothing to save the world from global warming by tacitly encouraging industries to move to non-Annex I countries. Although it may seem counterproductive, until the emissions markets mature and become transparent each industry and country should be allowed to take advantage of all the ways conceivable to hedge their liabilities.

France negotiated from a position of strength within the EU and does not have to make any cuts below 1990 emission levels. Notwithstanding the fact that emission levels in the power sector have in fact fallen, growth in transport has led to an average 1.4% growth in energy usage per year. Wood MacKenzie estimates that France will miss its emission target by 15% in 2010.[2] Most other European countries will be in worse shape.

In terms of energy efficiency, i.e. the comparison between the amount of CO_2 produced per unit of energy created, nobody in Europe does quite as badly as the Polish. This is a reflection of the high proportion of coal the country uses to generate electricity. Meeting Kyoto targets will be difficult for the country, despite the collapse in the economy after the painful transition from Communism to capitalism. Poland benchmarks

---

[2]   All figures relating to projected emissions in this chapter are drawn from various reports prepared by Wood Mackenzie. Wood Mackenzie, a consulting and research firm specializing in the energy sector, is a division of Deutsche Bank.

its emissions target against 1988 levels, but with the recovery of the economy and a resultant growth in energy usage in the transportation sector and an increase in power demands, Poland would be expected to overshoot its target by a considerable margin. To counteract this, there is a massive program to move from coal to gas in the upcoming years. All in all, Poland is expected to just meet its target of an 8% reduction of emissions.

Second only to Poland in the table of European polluters is Greece, which also relies on indigenous coal to meet its power demands. Greece could meet its Kyoto target if it converted its electricity generation to gas, but this is politically difficult. Continued growth in the transportation sector and continued high demands for electricity mean that Greece is likely to fall short of its target by over 16%, which is extraordinary given that the EU has allowed them to increase emissions by 25% from their 1990 level.

Just behind Greece in the league table is Denmark; the EU has targeted this country for a 21% reduction from 1990 levels. In the early 1990s, Denmark moved from being a net importer of electricity to a net exporter. Unfortunately, most of this power is produced from coal. Going forward, the government has proposed a massive move towards renewable energy as part of its Energy 21 plan. The aim is to have 12% of its power from renewable sources by 2005, and 35% by 2030. This, coupled with the expected move from coal towards gas, should help the country clean up its act, but currently it looks as though Denmark will miss its Kyoto target by 30%.

Ireland is ranked number four in the table of the least efficient energy users in Europe, producing about three tons of emissions for every ton of energy used. Ireland has always used the excuse that it is too poor a nation to avoid environmental investment, an argument that holds little weight after a decade of phenomenal economic growth. Ireland's dependence on coal and peat is being replaced slowly by gas supplied from Britain, but the transport and industrial sectors are pushing demand strongly. Ireland also has no nuclear capacity, and no other source of clean fuel. With economic growth expected to continue at a rapid rate, Ireland will miss its emissions target by almost 28% by 2010, even though the EU has allowed the country to increase emissions by 13% from 1990 figures.

The Czech Republic and Bulgaria will probably meet their 2010 targets, benefiting from a shift from coal- to gas-fired electrical generation. Both countries' economies collapsed after the end of Communism but have bounced back robustly, and they have been able to purchase modern gas turbines to meet increased power demands. The end of an era dominated by heavy industry and the start of a new era of light industrial production has meant that energy usage has dropped. Both countries have seen a rise in per capita incomes and a corresponding increase in automobile usage and growth in residential power consumption. Bulgaria set a target calling for an 8% reduction from 1988 levels and the Czech Republic set the goal at a similar reduction from 1989 levels. The Czech Republic is expected to fall under its target level by a comfortable margin of 13%, and Bulgaria is expected to emit less than 78% of its target level by 2010. These are two rather small countries that are sitting on excess credits.

Portugal, like Ireland, has made a tremendous economic leap in the past decade, and can no longer claim that poverty is an impediment against environmental investment. Portugal has been given the most leeway by the EU, which has allowed it to increase emissions by 27% from 1990 levels. Portugal has the "Watermelons", which is a political alignment linking the Green Party with the Communist Party. These two parties, when united, exert a great deal of political pressure on the government to meet clean air standards. At the same time, industry and the power sector have increased the use of oil and coal, resulting in a rapid growth in greenhouse gas emissions. Increased personal income has also led to explosive growth in the use of the car and greater demands for domestic electricity. Portugal will probably miss its Kyoto targets by over 45%.

Romania has invested heavily in nuclear power, and the newly commissioned Canadian reactor, Cernavoda, will come online early this decade. This will meet increased electrical demand and will allow the country to achieve its commitment to an 8% reduction on 1988 emissions. By the year 2010, Romania is only expected to reach 65% of its 1988 levels.

Luxembourg is being penalized unfairly because of gasoline tax differentials. Luxembourg's heavy industries have been in decline, which has contributed to a lowering in CO_2 emissions. The country also buys most of its electricity from France and Belgium, meaning that it is not accountable for any emissions from those sources. Luxembourg has one of the lowest gasoline taxes in Europe, however, and residents of neighboring countries think nothing of driving across the border to fill their tanks. As a result, the country is penalized for those emissions. If this were not the case, the country would easily meet its target. If Luxembourg does not decide to equalize its gasoline taxes in line with the rest of the EU, it will fall short of its ambitious emissions target by 31%. The EU has targeted the country for a 28% reduction in emissions by 2010.

Italy has one of the biggest economies and highest standards of living in Europe, and is expected to reduce emissions by 6% from 1990 levels by the year 2010. It has a strong industrial sector, but unlike its neighbor, France, it does not have any nuclear capacity. Italy uses very little coal in its power mix, relying heavily on cleaner burning natural gas. The country has exhausted all of its opportunities for expanding hydroelectric power, but it is toying with certain renewable options. Continued high demand for electrical power will push the country beyond its target level of emissions by 31%.

The environmental lobby in Austria has successfully stopped the country from initiating any further hydroelectric projects, at least for the time being. As a result the reliance on gas and coal for electrical generation will increase. Austria is one of the richest countries in Europe when judged by per capita income. In an increasingly sophisticated economy, heavy industry is being replaced by light industry, which is leading to a corresponding decrease in industrial demand for energy. Growth in the transportation sector has counterbalanced this drop and pushed up the level of growth in greenhouse gas emissions. As a result, Austria will miss its Kyoto target by about 28%. It has a goal of reducing emission by 13%.

Germany has the biggest economy, the highest standard of living and the largest environmental lobby in Europe. The Green Party often pushes through political policies that work against the country's effort to meet its emissions targets. As a result of this pressure, the country announced that it would retire its nuclear capacity over the course of the next two decades. If this is carried out, meeting future emission targets will prove impossible. Germany acquired a collapsed economy in eastern Europe, which brought with it a host of "hot air" credits. Restarting the economy in the east has proved more difficult than originally imagined, so energy demand across the country has grown slower than expected. Nevertheless, Germany will miss its target by at least 18% in 2010. Germany has the ambitious target of reducing emissions by 21% from 1990 levels.

Finland used to buy a lot of power from Russia, but the source of this cheap electricity is no longer reliable, and the country has had to build new coal- and gas-fired plants. This has led to a leap in emissions and a resultant investment in research to find ways to generate this power cleanly. Finland has been experimenting with hydrogen-powered generation, but this is a long way away from turning an experiment into a practical project. Finland will be pushed short of its target by almost 26%, even though the EU has allowed the country to keep emissions at a static level from the 1990 figure.

Spain has made the same across-the-board conversion from coal- to gas-generated electricity that the UK undertook in the last decade. This has led to a 15% drop in emissions in the power industry, but unfortunately this has been more than offset by a massive leap in demand from the transportation sector. Once again, a rise in per capita income has pushed people off public transport and into private vehicles, which is pushing up demand for gasoline by more than 2.5% per year. Spain will miss its Kyoto target by over 32%, even though the EU allowed the country a 15% increase from its 1990 levels.

The Netherlands has the "greenest image" in Europe, but this is simply a disguise covering one of the most successful economies in the world. The Dutch control a vast international network of businesses, ranging from flower distribution to energy. As a result, The Hague, Amsterdam and Rotterdam are huge sea and inland ports, from which vast quantities of materials are trans-shipped to other locations. A large portion of the deliveries made by the Dutch are made overland by heavy trucks to other European cities, which creates strong annual growth for both diesel fuel and gasoline. At the same time, the Green lobby in the Netherlands has successfully pushed for the retirement of its nuclear generators, which has counterbalanced the country's successful shift from coal to gas. Power demand is growing by about 5% a year, laying the ground for a shortfall of approximately 25% for the country's 2010 Kyoto targets. The Netherlands has been targeted to reduce emissions by only 6% from 1990 levels.

Belgium is expected to exceed targets by almost 21%, even though their reduction target is only 7.5%. The figure would have been much higher if the country had not made a big switch from coal- to gas-fired generation. The main growth area for emissions in Belgium is from the transport sector.

Switzerland has a big nuclear and hydroelectric industry, which ensures that power generation accounts for few of its emissions. About 70% of the emissions that the country produces are from petroleum products, primarily gasoline and diesel fuel used for personal and commercial transport. Power generation accounts for only about 10% of Switzerland's total greenhouse gas emissions. The astounding growth in the transport sector means that the country will miss its Kyoto target by 17%.

Slovakia has recovered well from the collapse of Communism and is developing an economy to rival its neighbor, the Czech Republic. Economic growth is expected to continue at a rate above 4% per annum into the next decade, but emissions are rising only slightly. This is due to an across-the-board conversion from coal to gas, and a big investment in nuclear power. Heavy industry has been replaced by more efficient light industries, which has offset a growth in demand for power from the residential sector. Slovakia will meet its target by a healthy margin, and will probably benefit from trading some of these credits with EU countries.

Hungary is another successful post-Communist society, and one of the countries earmarked for EU membership in this decade. Correspondingly, the growth in emissions has rivaled its economic performance. Electrification at the time of the conversion to a market economy was not complete in Hungary, so the country has had to adapt to an increase in demand from a growing residential sector. Coal still plays a major part in the energy mix, although natural gas use is also growing. Hungary intelligently chose to set its target at a 6% reduction from 1985–1987 levels, when heavy industry dominated the economy. As a result, the country will meet target levels by a healthy margin of 13%.

Norway and Sweden have entirely different emissions scenarios, although both will miss their Kyoto targets by wide margins. Norway relies heavily on hydroelectric power, and exports a lot of this emission-free energy. All Norway has to do is meet a target that allows for an increase of 1% over 1990 levels, but it will fall far short of this due primarily to an increase in demand for petroleum products from the transport sector and growing domestic demand for power. Norway will be out of the target range for 2010 by over 42% unless drastic action is taken to reduce emissions. Norway's government was the first to fall as a result of political dissent that has erupted because of a commitment to comply with the Kyoto Protocol. The government was opposed to the construction of new gas-powered electricity generators on the basis that it would increase national emissions of CO_2. An investigative report published in an Oslo newspaper, *Dagsavisen*, revealed government plans to ration electricity in the future if voluntary programs to reduce consumption failed. The government was forced to resign on 8 March 2000 as a result of the crisis. Sweden is suffering because of a hyperactive environmental lobby dedicated to shutting down its nuclear capacity and limiting the introduction of new hydroelectric projects. The Swedes were expected to meet their targets if they had been allowed to exploit emissions-free energy resources, but by instituting the environmentalists' agenda, the country will miss its goal of reducing emissions by about 39%. Under EU rules it was supposed to reduce emissions by 4% during this period.

Turkey, although not technically a European country, is vying for EU membership and is expected to take a different political stance towards the Kyoto Protocol in this decade. The country is still developing, and its economy has been shaken to the core by recent natural disasters. Nevertheless, it has a growing middle class who are increasingly environmentally aware. The country still has a goal of raising living standards across the board, and energy demands are growing at a rapid rate. If Turkey had a Kyoto target based upon 1990 levels, they would exceed that by 78%.

The Japanese also possess a "green" image, greatly enhanced by hosting the COP-3 meeting in Kyoto, which resulted in an agreement to mandate cuts globally among Annex I countries. Japan was given a target of reducing emissions by 6% from 1990 levels. Despite a commitment to lower emissions and increase energy efficiency, the Japanese are expected to miss their target by at least 16%. This is a deliberately conservative figure that relies on the growth of the nuclear capability of the country, as well as increased efficiencies gained by new gas turbine technology.

On the whole, Europe's position towards meeting its Kyoto commitments is not much better than that of the USA. On a country-by-country basis, there are few examples where political commitments are translating into reality. The UK actually reduced emissions across the board by 5% between 1990 and 1995, but many people expect it to still fall short of its ambitious goal to cut emissions substantially from 1990 levels. By sector, industry in Europe will remain relatively stable in terms of emissions. The European residential and transportation sectors will emit about 10% and 25% more emissions, respectively. Throughout Europe, the transportation sector is leading demand for energy and making the problem of reducing greenhouse gases seemingly irresolvable. There are significant areas for improvement, however, and these can be done painlessly. Even by the year 2010, it is estimated that Europe will still be emitting 747 000 tons of CO_2 as a result of burning coal. A conversion to gas across the board would reduce this figure by about one-third, and stepping up nuclear generation to replace coal-burning capacity would eliminate the emissions caused by burning coal. The problem lies not with the willingness of governments, but with political resistance brought to bear by the environmental lobby. In many cases, concerns about the effects of nuclear and hydroelectric power are getting in the way of solving the problems of global warming.

Of all the countries who could possibly meet the Kyoto targets, the UK is best placed, closely followed by Germany, France and Belgium. The EU is planning to implement a program that allows trading of emissions by 2005. The problem is that there are few, if any, emission credits available for trading. The Baltic states have committed to meeting the same targets as the EU, but Russia is the country sitting on the most available credits. It is doubtful that the EU will recognize their validity, though, and their excess credits are not enough to let the rest of the Annex I countries meet their targets. The UK and Denmark have both set up preliminary trading schemes. Denmark has already begun to cap emissions in the energy sector.

If the EU allows trading only within the bloc in 2005, the results will be dismal. The lack of available credits will drive prices too high. Without the inclusion of other countries, there will be little incentive for European companies to trade. The EU will have to do something drastic to meet targets, or go on to the open markets and buy over 600 million tons of CO_2 credits. The EU knows how unrealistic this would be, and has decided the best method for reaching their targets is to tax fossil fuels heavily, thereby discouraging their use.

The lack of political resistance to the Kyoto Protocol in Europe cannot be attributed solely to an increased environmental awareness among the electorate. Europeans are no greener than Americans are; they just operate under a different political system that allows for less dissent. As demonstrated by the spate of demonstrations across Europe in September 2000 against the high price of diesel fuel and gasoline, there is growing resistance to punitive taxation. Europeans may harbor the same environmental sentiments as Americans, and feel an even greater necessity to stop global warming, but they are not yet aware of the burden of costs that will be imposed upon them. The American system of government allows for greater examination of the impact of new regulations prior to enactment. The reason the Americans have not rushed into ratification of the Kyoto Protocol at the same pace as the Europeans is that their political system is geared to spawn debate and dissent, not just between various political factions but also internally within both major political parties. The environmental benefit of legislation in America is always weighed against the economic impact. The added burden of taxation that will be imposed upon Europeans as a result of the ratification of the Kyoto Protocol would not be tolerated in America unless it was presented in a different manner. Americans would tolerate a specific tax for a specific period of time if it were designed solely to develop alternative technologies. Americans would not consent to a series of punitive taxes intended to "shape" public behavior.

Although they are loath to admit it, the French are much more like the Americans than any other European nationality. France stands to gain more out of the battle to fight global warming than any other nation besides America. The technology the nation develops is in many respects far ahead of what comes out of the USA, and much of this will be used globally to develop the basic infrastructure to reduce greenhouse gas emissions. On an individual basis, the French also have no problem expressing their dissent and stopping government legislation in its tracks. The government of France is about to arbitrarily impose a new series of taxes on its people that will make the latest series of fuel price increases seem like small change. Although the intent of reducing emissions is well founded, this will be a punitive tax designed solely to discourage the burning of fossil fuels. As France does not burn nearly the same amount of fossil fuels to generate power as other countries, their main target has to be the transportation sector.

Just like Americans, the French view their cars as extensions of their personal freedom. And, just like the Americans, the French are more concerned with their personal freedom than they are with government authority. When the government arbitrarily decides that the only solution to global warming is to infringe the liberty of its own people, its days will be numbered. If, on the other hand, the French government proposed an investment strategy that used public funds to lead the world in the creation of new technologies, develop domestic infrastructure and create new jobs, the potential for political resistance would diminish substantially.

The EU is about to go out on a long limb, and the political risk it is taking is enormous. Ratification of the Kyoto Protocol, without a corresponding commitment from the USA, just lays the seed for an eventual political reaction that halts the process in its tracks. A host of new taxes is about to be imposed on individuals and industry without a corresponding program of investment that would eventually resolve the problem. Rather than boldly taking the lead in developing solutions to the problem, the EU is deciding that the only answer lies in lowering the standard of living for its citizens. There is no Cooler Heads Coalition in Europe that exists to point out the real cost of environmental action, and that acts as a catalyst to debate. Any commitment as far reaching as the EU is about to embark upon requires broad-based support. The fact that opposition to ratification of the Kyoto Protocol is muted at present does not mean there is universal support for the implementation of a program of emission cuts that drive industry away and increase the cost of personal transportation. Europe may currently be far "greener" than the USA, but when the costs of idealism are finally added up, the shade of this green may well lighten considerably.

4

POWER TO THE PEOPLE

In the blame game there is typically only one rule of thumb, and that is that the individual never bears any responsibility. This is a phenomenal way of thinking, particularly when it relates to global warming. All responsibility can be placed solely on the back of the industrial sector that produces goods such as automobiles and electricity and, in the process, pollutes the atmosphere. No responsibility falls on the back of the innocent individuals that buy the cars or use the electricity, as they are obviously not intelligent enough to know that they are intrinsic to the entire process. They are merely victims in an evil game. Fortunately, this way of thinking is not quite universal. There are certain places in the world where intelligence reigns and individuals take responsibility for their own actions, and this is particularly true if you drive west, just past the Nevada border.

The relationship between companies and individuals is exceedingly simple. Occasionally, perhaps as the result of heavy advertising, we may deviate a fraction, but on the whole companies produce what we want. Put simply, companies are in the business of satisfying our desires. Global warming is really a result of individuals' desires for convenience and luxury. We want powerful cars rather than efficient cars. We worry more about having instantaneous hot water than conserving energy. Since we have only just discovered global warming, it is more than a little disingenuous to blame businesses that have been providing for our needs, and polluting the atmosphere as a result, for the past century.

Just as the EU model of sneaking in a range of punitive taxes to shape public behavior is doomed to failure, there is a different model for change that brings with it a guarantee of success. Any effort to confront a problem as massive and important as this requires an extraordinary public concern and reaction. The key driver to change is people. Governments cannot institute change in vacuums, and business can be made to solve the problem only when the general public demands it.

In 1965, Ralph Nader published *Unsafe at Any Speed*, a book that was highly critical of the design and safety features of certain models of American cars. The book was widely read and created a public stir that was translated almost instantly into legislative action. Despite the howls from the automobile manufacturing industry, which claimed the changes would be too expensive, televised public hearings were held, legislation was drafted, and safety regulations were implemented. Three years earlier, Rachel Carson had written and published *Silent Spring*, a book that revealed the link between the widespread use of DDT for insect control and the devastating effect it was having on the bird and fish population in America. Once again, public reaction was swift and the offending pesticides were banned from use. In the case of DDT, the farming community insisted that crop yields would fall as a result of DDT being prohibited, but industry responded by coming up with replacement substances that did not harm wildlife. After Nader's book was published, the automobile industry quickly began to incorporate safety features into the design of new cars, and automobile deaths were cut as a result.

There will probably be no seminal work about climate change that will wake up the collective consciousness of the public and spur the same sort of instantaneous reaction from the government. The problem is too subtle and too complex, and enough concrete evidence does not yet exist to write about the subject with any real authority. A scientific treatise packed with correlations will lack the passion required to motivate voter concern. Global warming is not primarily a health concern, or even so much of an environmental concern, as it is a moral concern. The public will not be won over by an environmental argument or a scientific argument, but if global warming is presented as a moral issue the public will begin to exert influence on government. The intervention of EU and American troops in such far-flung locations as Sierra Leone, Kosovo and Somalia had nothing to do with security concerns. These actions were taken and received broad support because the public saw a clear distinction between morality and immorality.

At the moment, the issue of climate change occupies just a few lines of a party platform or manifesto, but it is not something that has been dealt with yet by a special address from the president or Prime Minister. The populations of the Annex I countries have in no way been mobilized or even informed at a high level about the seriousness of the problem. This process will start soon, and it will stir up concern and provoke a contentious debate about the issue in the media. Most importantly, it will get people thinking. Many of them will get behind the process and push through positive political action. For this to work, strong scientific evidence will have to be provided, which states climate change is a real problem. The hard part will come next: setting an agenda and turning it into legislative action.

Industry can fight battles in the halls of the Capitol building in Washington, and it can sometimes win, but industry can never win when faced with an outraged public. A smart company will always try to stay one step ahead of the consumer, and will attempt to anticipate how the mood of the people is going to change. A good example of this is the rebranding of bP, where the letters that once stood for "British Petroleum" now stand for "Beyond Petroleum". It is all too easy to be cynical about this, as a number of environmental groups have been, but the reality is that bP is one of the most successful companies in the world, and got there by giving people what they want.

During a speech to the Aluminum Association in Washington, Paul O'Neil, the former CEO of Alcoa, spoke of global warming as a problem that would have a $3 trillion a year impact on the global economy. He recommended that governments adopt a virtual wartime footing to deal with the problem, explore every scientific option, educate the public and do everything possible to stop the process. He likened the crisis to the prospect of nuclear holocaust. He spoke as both a head of one of America's largest companies and a concerned individual, worried about the sort of environment his children and grandchildren would inherit. These were powerful words from a senior business executive, and a former senior government official in the executive branch under Kennedy, Johnson, Nixon and Ford. As he was speaking to an industry association composed of some of the biggest greenhouse gas emitters in the world, he said all the right things. But what the audience particularly liked was his solution to the problem. According to O'Neil, the problem could be solved "without the overhanging threat of a government pounding us into submission or bribing us to do things we ought to do anyway."[1]

O'Neil's solution to the problem was a call for "voluntary action", which is sweet music to the heads of major corporations. The prospect of voluntary action presents an ideal opportunity for a utility to stick a picture of a windmill on their annual report, and thereby claim they are doing their bit to reduce greenhouse gases without big government hanging over their shoulder. The same can be said for an automobile manufacturer or an energy company. The problem of course is that voluntary action will never happen unless there is pressure from the public or the government.

[1]   Speech given to the Aluminum Association by Paul O'Neill, Washington, DC, 6 March 1998.

In 1970, the US Congress passed the Clean Air Act, which was a landmark response to a public outpouring of environmental concern prompted by the first Earth Day. This bill was thrown together and passed so quickly that industry was unable to mount a significant defense. Congress have since learned their lesson, and are now much better at public relations. Hence, the valiant call for voluntary action by industry to prevent the horrors of climate change. If they are successful they can hold off legislative action for up to a decade, while the atmosphere continues to degrade at an ever-increasing rate. By that time, there will be no other choice but to bring in a strong set of laws, because pressure on the legislature will be brought to bear by the mounting concerns of the electorate.

Broad-based voter-inspired environmental pressure works. The French took one of the most polluted bodies of water in Europe, Lake Annecy, and turned it into the cleanest lake on the continent. The French and Swiss combined efforts to clean up Lake Geneva and revive commercial fishing on the water. The residents of the states surrounding the Great Lakes in the USA worked together with the Canadian province of Ontario to clean up water pollution that was flowing into this body of water from its tributaries. These actions were all inspired by voters' concerns. In all of these cases, voter pressure forced industry to change the types of products it produced. The French forced the makers of outboard motors to develop lower horsepower engines. The USA and Canada forced tankers to stop the practice of emptying their bilge tanks into the lake water. Pressure was brought to bear in France, Canada, Switzerland and the USA on the makers of fertilizers to reduce the sales of phosphates in areas that would run off into bodies of fresh water. These initiatives did not originate in the legislative bodies of these countries, but rose out of the ranks of voters and environmental pressure groups that represented them.

If we want a model for positive legislative action we have to look no further than California. The reasons are obvious: over 90% of the state's regions do not meet federal air quality standards, and some of the areas are so bad that it is visibly harmful to the health to take a deep breath. This is not a new problem: the first smog alert occurred in Los Angeles in 1943 and was originally thought to be a poison gas attack by the Japanese.[2] The problem with global warming is that it is not visible, and it will take a few years for people to feel its effect. But smog is very visible and literally gets right up the taxpayers' noses. Solely because the environment in California has degraded to such an extent, conservation and environmental concerns are uniquely bipartisan issues in the state. The opinions of the Democratic Party and the Republican Party on such issues as fiscal policy, minority rights and immigration may be poles apart in California, but the environmental stance of the two parties is virtually the same.[3] These policies are not driven by the party apparat, but are born from grass roots concerns. If you can taste the air, and its color is orange, it is motivation enough to make your way to the polls to cast your vote for the candidate who promises to turn it blue again.

Even before the US government passed the Clean Air Act, Californians were already in on the game and had identified the main culprit. In the mid-1960s, the state had already set its target on the four-wheeled monster and was calling for an end to leaded gasoline. The US auto industry resisted strongly, claiming that the installation of catalytic converters in automobiles was expensive and impractical. The Swedes broke ranks, though, and instantly began selling Volvos fitted with the devices, and the rest of the industry quickly found out it was not such a big prob-

[2]   Thanks to a colossal effort, Houston has now overtaken Los Angeles as the city in America with the worst air quality.

[3]   Pete Wilson, the former Governor of California, was a conservative Republican, but a strong environmentalist. Individuals such as Jan Sharpliss, the former Chairwoman of the Air Resources Board, were also conservative Republicans, but not afraid to stand up to industry to fight for the environment.

lem after all. The installation of the catalytic converter became mandatory throughout the USA subsequent to the Californians' action. California has in fact co-opted out of US environmental action because its local policies are much more stringent than federal regulations.

The emphasis on the car and the damage it does to the atmosphere applies not just to local smog; it is also important in the issue of global warming because the automobile is the biggest single man-made source of greenhouse gas emissions.[4] California's experience in shaping legislation to create environmentally friendly solutions to problems should be a lesson to the rest of the world. California is a big enough market to single-handedly mandate the development of a whole new set of products that not only lower smog levels but also reduce greenhouse gases. Most importantly, the voters of California have no fear of telling industry what to do, and have no compunction about shutting companies out of the market that do not comply with their mandates.

The 1988 California Clean Air Act set up the Air Resources Board, which set the agenda for the most ambitious plan in the world to reduce car pollution. They set as a goal for 1998 that at least 10% of the new cars sold in the state would be "zero-emission" vehicles. Industry rebelled instantly and convinced the board to put the date for implementation back to 2003. This was accepted on the basis that a further five years' developmental time was required for industry to innovate a new type of vehicle that would be accepted by the public. At the time the Air Resources Board mandated change, industry did not have the technology to meet the challenge. The voters of California effectively forced the car makers of the world to develop an entirely new product, and, to their credit, they are succeeding. These new cars will be the saviors of the world.

If there is one group of environmentalists in the world that can be

[4] Automotive exhaust not only accounts for the emission of one third of CO_2, but is also the fastest growing source of greenhouse gases.

trusted, they are the Union of Concerned Scientists (UCS). Judging solutions from a rational rather than emotive perspective inspires confidence from the public. The research conducted by Roland Hwang, who runs transportation research for the group, has done much to affect policy in California towards the automobile. Hwang's ambition is to "decarbonize the California economy", and to simultaneously create economic growth. To the uninitiated, the two do not seem to go hand in hand, but in practice the leadership position the state has taken will ensure that its emission-reducing technology will have an international market in the coming decades.

America unfortunately has a love affair with the sports utility vehicle (SUV), which is leading the country down the road to wrack and ruin. According to figures from the UCS, the average SUV emits 9.1 tons of greenhouse gases a year, as opposed to 6.4 tons for the average car. If SUVs were eliminated entirely, the USA would be able to reduce total CO_2 emissions by 237 million tons, as well as saving 18.4 billion gallons of gasoline a year. At an average price of $15 a barrel for crude oil, the savings in imported oil would amount to almost $7 billion. If the cost of CO_2 emissions was factored in, the value of this cut in emissions would be worth over $3.5 billion.[5] These are all rational arguments that might prompt government action in another country to control the manufacture and sales of these vehicles, but America is a different place. Americans are not about to be told that it is their environmental responsibility to trade in their four-wheel drive behemoth for an aluminum and plastic mini car. A different solution has to be found, and California is working on it. It is the goal of California to make the SUV not just more fuel efficient but also emission free; the impact of this would be enormous. If they can prompt this action, making a normal car emission free is fairly straightforward.

There is a starting point in all this, and Californians have begun with

[5]   Calculated at a price of $15/ton.

the "City Car", or the "50–50 car".[6] The voters have essentially forced this technology upon the auto companies, and although it flies in the face of the American concept of bigger is better, it is considered a good starting point for developing the zero emission car. The City Car is designed for two groups: teenagers and retirees. It is known as the "50–50 car" because it has a maximum speed of 50 mph and a range of 50 miles between charging. Ford was the first auto company to respond to popular voter pressure, by buying a Norwegian company that produced a lightweight electric car with an aluminum frame and plastic body panels. They renamed the car "Think" for the American market. Under the complicated system by which the state judges compliance with the Clean Air Act (which requires that every car company's sales be at least 10% zero emission vehicles), the City Car counts as a whole unit. The problem with the City Car is it is a niche market product. Battery-powered cars are not produced in significant enough volume to be competitively priced, but they make up some of the price difference by the lower cost of power and maintenance. The state recognizes this and is willing to give car companies some leeway to attract a mainstream audience.

The next step up from the City Car is the more advanced electric vehicle with nickel–cadmium batteries. These cars have a range of up to 140 miles, although their appeal is still limited. The only car with potential mass appeal that begins to meet state standards at present is the "hybrid". This car would not exist if California had not demanded its production.[7]

[6] It can be argued that electric cars that require recharging only transfer the source of pollution from the tail pipe to a distant electrical generator. This is true to some extent, but even factoring in the pollution produced by the generating plant, the greenhouse gas emissions of a battery car are 70% less than that of a normal car with the same power and range powered by an internal combustion engine.

[7] Although the Japanese version of the hybrid car was designed specifically for the American market, it is in fact much more popular in Japan than in California.

The hybrid car is electric powered, but is assisted by either an internal combustion engine or a fuel cell. The Chevrolet Triax car, once again built specifically for the Californian market, is the world's first "modular" car. The drive train is electric and batteries power it, but these batteries are charged either by small combustion engines or fuel cells. The auxiliary engine can be replaced depending on whether the vehicle is sold in an area that meets federally approved air standards or falls short of those standards. These cars have no ultimate limit on their range and can obtain excellent fuel efficiencies. Honda's "Insight" hybrid is expected to run at 70 miles per gallon, giving it a range of 700 miles on a tank of gasoline. They will be priced competitively priced against conventional vehicles and will cut emissions of global warming gases by up to one-third or even a half. As these cars fall short of the state-mandated target, but still reduce pollutants, each sale of a hybrid is valued at three-tenths of the sale of a zero emission vehicle.

There is a final category that provides car companies with some credit towards the goal of attaining 10% zero emission sales. These cars are called "super ultra low emitting vehicles" (SULEVs). They use conventional internal combustion engines that are so efficient that their emissions are a fraction of that of a normal car. Under state rules, a sale of a SULEV is valued at one-fifth of the sale of a zero emission car.

Breaking the American love affair with the SUV is an impossible goal for California, but they are trying to make this car as green as is possible. Under the arcane rules that govern federally mandated fuel economy standards, the SUV is counted not as a passenger car but as a light truck. This category of vehicle includes business vans and industrial trucks that are required to perform heavier work and thus cannot meet the same efficiency standards as a family car. The federal government requires that each auto maker's portfolio of cars obtain an average fuel efficiency of 27.5 miles per gallon. Light trucks are required to achieve a standard of only 20.7 miles per gallon. As California is exempted from federal air quality rules, they are free to take this government standard and improve upon it. Their plan to make the SUV emissions free is openly disingenuous. Their real intention is to legislate them off the roads.

General Motors is planning to release a small SUV hybrid car in 2003. In a joint venture with Toyota, the Pontiac division of the company is building a prototype car called the "Escape". This hybrid will be fitted with either a fuel cell or a small internal combustion engine. The credit for each sale will be limited to one-fifth of the value of a zero emission car. The car companies are only allowed to reach up to 60% of their obligation for zero emission car sales by using partial credits.

The state of California and the federal government have disagreements about the use of diesel fuel. Once again, the voters of Southern California do not want to increase particulate pollution, but the federal government is keen to convert a significant portion of the heavy truck fleet to diesel as a means of reducing CO_2 emissions. Global warming is not a voter issue in California. The residents of San Francisco and Los Angeles are concerned only with local smog. Recent studies conducted in the state have linked particulate pollution with cancer. The voters decided to override federal mandates and ban the sale of diesel-powered vehicles by the year 2004.

In order to promote the sale of greener products, California toyed with the idea of a revenue neutral tax that subsidized nonpolluting products and penalized products that were obviously bad for the environment. Although the design of the tax plan was supposed to be revenue neutral, realistically it was expected to generate some income, which the state wanted to pump back into the public transportation system. The vote was opposed by an unlikely coalition of liberals, who were concerned about the effect the tax would have on the poor, and the conservatives, who did not want to introduce a new tax on the rich.

To solve the problem of global warming we need two things. We need industry to supply solutions, and we need people to buy them. Retiring the internal combustion engine is not an easy task. When a gallon of gasoline in California is cheaper than a two-liter bottle of mineral water, there is little incentive to switch to alternative fuels or for car makers to invest in untested technologies. Pressure has to be brought to bear on the industrial sector to change their product lines, either directly by the people or indirectly via legislation. If legislation is imposed on an unwilling public to correct a problem they do not recognize, the laws will be ignored or flouted. If, on the other hand, the demand for legislative action arises from the grass roots the laws will be welcomed.

The solutions for the power sector and the industrial sector are clear. For the individuals of the world, who are responsible for emitting more greenhouse gases than industry, they are equally obvious. We can stop global warming in its tracks by a few simple changes, and these changes will make life better for us all.

In the following chapters, we will examine the solutions or proposed solutions to global warming, and then look at how the financial markets can be mobilized to address this problem. There are many vested interests, some with very strong agendas, that want to shape the way the world focuses its efforts to stop the process of climate change. Our views are equally contentious, but we think they are realistic and present the world with the greatest opportunity to continue on the path towards economic growth, whilst significantly reducing the amount of greenhouse gases the world emits into the atmosphere.

5

THE AFTERBURNERS

Some people are absolutely convinced that there are still ways in which we can fight global warming, even assuming the world is going to continue to burn fossil fuels to generate power and drive transport. Quite reasonably, this school of thought is based on the premise that it would be rash to throw away the infrastructure that provides the earth's inhabitants with the warmth, transport and luxury they want. The aim of this group, who we refer to as the Afterburners, is to tackle the problem of what happens after fossil fuel is burnt. There are two ways to approach the problem: coerce nature to absorb CO_2 naturally, or capture CO_2 at source and store it in some way.

These are actually two radically different approaches. If nature can be coerced to absorb CO_2, this gives us all the leeway we need to carry on as we are. The other alternative would have applications limited strictly to fixed places where CO_2 is produced in quantities, such as power stations, and where expensive technology could be put into place that would somehow capture emissions at the smoke stack and pump them back into the ground.

The underlying element in all of this is carbon. Carbon enters the global warming food chain as a fossil fuel (i.e. a hydrocarbon), which is burnt to generate power, which produces CO_2. The CO_2 is then absorbed by vegetation or enters the oceans as carbonates. At no point is carbon itself created or destroyed; it simply combines itself with other elements, such as hydrogen or oxygen, to produce gases, liquids and solids. To make calculations simpler, the basic unit we will use will be one gigaton of carbon.[1] Just as it would be difficult to imagine having a million dollars in a suitcase, we find it hard to picture the size of a gigaton of carbon, so we will refer to one gigaton of carbon as one unit.

It is important to understand the dynamics of carbon flows, particularly if you buy into the idea of using nature to store the excess carbon we produce. Each year the human race throws about eight units of carbon into the air, of which 6.5 units come from the burning of fossil fuels and other manufacturing processes and 1.5 units are created by land use change. About 3.2 units stay in the atmosphere; the remainder is absorbed in roughly equal proportions by the terrestrial vegetation and the oceans. These figures are quite dramatic, but behind these net changes there are many more complex things going on. For instance, there is a continual interchange of carbon between terrestrial vegetation and the atmosphere of about 110 units per year, which makes the eight units we throw into the atmosphere every year seem like small potatoes. The Afterburners are convinced that we can solve the problem by altering the formula that exists in nature for the absorption of carbon. The basis for their way of thinking is that the current trade-off occurring naturally can be hiked up to some extent. Currently, about 108 units of carbon are given out by plants and soil by way of respiration,[2] and 110 units are absorbed by vegetation during photosynthesis. Similarly, there

---

[1]   One gigaton (Gt) is one billion (one thousand million) tons. One ton of carbon is approximately equivalent to four tons of CO_2. Therefore, when we say that the world produces around 6 GtC from various sources, this is similar to saying 24 billion tons of CO_2.

[2]   Excluding the extra 1.5 units coming from land use change.

is an interchange between the atmosphere and the ocean: the ocean gives up 102 units but absorbs about 104 units. To top it off, carbon moves around continuously between the surface of the ocean and the deep ocean troughs. Anyone with a head for figures and a deft hand at tinkering with nature will immediately grasp the potential here. If the formula for the natural interchange of carbon can be altered, we can "bank" the excess carbon we produce each year in one of two natural reservoirs – the vegetation or the oceans – and it can lie there for the "benefit" of future generations.

The least intrusive "storage" depot for carbon is vegetation, but this is about as unreliable as asking a child to guard the candy. Under the terms of the Kyoto Protocol, Annex I countries are allowed to use "land use change"[3] as a way of meeting their carbon reduction commitments. The thinking behind this is that trees naturally absorb CO_2, so planting more of them will offset emissions. It sounds like a pretty neat idea, and as everyone loves a tree, it is also a pretty painless solution. For the countries that have little chance of meeting their reduction targets, this sounds too good to be true and, for once, they are right. Nevertheless, it is the one battlefield against climate change that has already attracted significant interest and money right from the very beginning. There is not much involved with planting a forest, and if there is money to be made out of it, it sounds even better. Before the gavel is pounded to mark the end of the COP-3 meeting, funds have already been established and investments been made in distant locations to set up green carbon storage depots. Our Australian friends are way ahead of the pack in this area, and for them there are numerous beneficial side effects. The Kyoto Protocol provided them with an immediate and free way to reforest the land they had raped and plundered in previous generations. Australia has a surprisingly fragile ecosystem, and this was severely impacted when standing forests were chopped down in the early 1900s. The root structures of the

---

[3]   The full label is Land Use, Land-Use Change, and Forestry (LULUCF).

trees had soaked up the rainfall and kept the water table at a certain level for centuries. But when the forest cover was removed, the water table rose, bringing about an inevitable increase in the salinity of the soil. Government-financed reforestation was on the cards anyway, but the international community has now been motivated to do this on the government's behalf.

Because of the importance of forests in the overall carbon equation, the IPCC was asked to prepare a report on land use change for policy makers. Unfortunately their conclusions were not what everyone wanted to hear. In particular, the IPCC states:

> Ecosystem models indicate that the additional terrestrial uptake of atmospheric carbon dioxide arising from indirect effects of human activities on a global scale is likely to be maintained for a number of decades in forest ecosystems, *but may gradually diminish and forest ecosystems may even become a source.*[4]

What this report states is that planting a forest to recapture carbon in the atmosphere may work for a while, but it is not a static system, and the dynamics are such that the forests may eventually become sources of CO_2 rather than a storage depot. They cite a number of reasons for this, including:

> . . . the rate of photosynthesis in some types of plants may no longer increase as carbon dioxide concentration begins to rise, whereas heterotrophic respiration is expected to rise with increasing temperatures.

The usual assumption is that when CO_2 increases, this encourages photosynthesis, which brings the system back into balance, a fact that the report throws doubt upon. In addition, the report warns that as

---

[4]   Quoted from the *Land Use, Land-Use Change, and Forestry* report prepared by the IPCC in 2000.

temperatures rise, we could find that the entire ecosystem becomes damaged and plant respiration increases.

The report also warns that our understanding of climactic constraints and feedback processes is weak, and so projecting beyond a few decades is highly uncertain. But even on shorter timescales there is such wide disagreement between various scientific projections that we have to realize that while the overall direction of the predictions is probably realistic, the magnitudes are less clear.

Despite the reservations of the IPCC, the bandwagon is rolling on, and there are a number of heavyweight countries on board, all of whom are united in finding a cheap and easy way out of the problem. Many think the report, which questioned the positive effects of land use change, was toned down as the result of behind-the-scenes arm-twisting from the USA, Canada, Russia, Australia and New Zealand.

This IPCC report was put together to help in the up-and-coming COP-6 discussions in The Hague. In a sense, the fact that they have to have discussions, attended by hundreds of policy makers, to decide on a mutually acceptable definition for the word "forest" should give us a sense of the insanity of it all. We assume that a committee will be formed, which will appoint a subcommittee to determine what in fact constitutes a "tree". The matter will be handed out to an outside consulting firm and the process will grind to a halt until the question is ultimately resolved.

All the questions about the value of land use change come down to one thing: how to get value out of nothing. Whether it is not tilling the soil, or replanting a forest that was just cut down, twisting the laws of economics to fit the Kyoto Protocol makes a mockery of the entire process. Rather than take our word for it, we should provide you with an example of the importance of the outcome of these negotiations. A forest is often assessed in terms of its canopy cover, in other words how much light it lets in. If this is set too high, then large areas of more sparsely populated woodland can be cleared away without any effect on the country's carbon accounts. On the other hand, if it is set too low, then we could clear every second tree in the rainforests without a word being said against it. The decision of whether to save a particular forest or "harvest" it, or even to plant a tree, should not be predicated by global warming issues, but should be a decision based upon aesthetics or a respect for the beauty of nature.

"Land use change" can cover a pretty broad range of activities, and has been interpreted in myriad ways. A farmer that tills the soil exposes the root structure of living plants and thus emits CO_2 into the atmosphere. The farmer does this in order to plant new crops that capture more carbon. It is to all intents and purposes a carbon neutral situation, or at least it is to the layperson with a bit of common sense.

There is a school of thought out there that claims that by reducing the number of times a farmer tills the soil, the amount of carbon that is emitted into the atmosphere is reduced. Of course, this solution was never considered seriously until money entered the equation. At that stage, logic and common sense were turned on their heads by a little scientific sleight of hand. In theory they are right, but common sense tells us they are way off base.

If we look at the underlying facts about carbon stored in vegetation and soil, the landmass of the world is a vast storage depot that currently holds about 2477 units,[5] of which the soil accounts on average for some 80% of this. But more importantly we find that even at the extreme, the soil in tropical forests accounts for 50% of the carbon held, while at the other end of the scale, in croplands the soil accounts for 98% of the carbon retained. To assume that this figure has any meaning requires a leap of logic that is beyond us, but people will be tempted to distort the importance of this statistic to demonstrate the value of keeping the carbon stored in farmland underground as long as possible.

[5]   These figures come from the *Land Use, Land-Use Change, and Forestry* report prepared by the IPCC in 2000.

Everyone knows that a farmer overturns the land in order to plant new crops. The farmer may kill existing vegetation in the process, and this may decompose, but he is planting new crops on top of this that recapture carbon emitted into the air. This is done season after season, year after year. The decomposing crops act as fertilizer for the new crops, and these nutrients are brought up out of the ground to build plant fiber. Tinkering with this equation, and assuming that it stops carbon emissions from going into the atmosphere, would only be sold to a gullible public if money were involved.

To use such an extreme interpretation of land use change for profit definitely falls into the category of exploiting loopholes. Even if we were to concede that farmers should be paid to reduce the number of times they till the soil, the reality is that it would be a one-off payment. And to be entitled to that payment, the farmers would have to change their practices not just this year but forever.

The ocean holds over 20 times as much carbon as does terrestrial vegetation, and so it has naturally attracted some serious attention. It would have been the focus of much more research had the funding been available. The problem is that the practical problems of doing the research and proving you have done it are immense, and without the accounting there is no money to be made, and therefore no sponsorship to be had. So while this has reduced the attention on this area it has not kept away some of the world's more imaginative scientists.

First of all, we have no real understanding of the dynamics of ocean vegetation, and how photosynthesis and respiration work on the surface or deep under water. When we look at the oceans, we need to consider a host of variables, all of which interact with each other. It would probably require a few centuries of time on a Cray supercomputer plus a host of data we do not have to model the changes that occur naturally. The transfer of carbon between the surface, deep waters and ocean sediments, the effect this has on various types of animal and plant life, the relative concentration of various nutrients such as iron and nitrates, and the fact that the main currents take thousands of years to traverse the world are all matters we may understand separately but have no idea as to how they work as a whole. It has to be said that the authors of this book do not know how all this works, and from what we have read we suspect that no-one else does either. But that does not stop people dreaming up fantastic ideas that could have untold side effects. The most amazing of these involves fertilizing the ocean with phosphates, nitrates and iron, or dissolving lime into the ocean in order to accelerate the absorption of CO_2.

The problem with all these ideas, and there are a lot of them, is that they will upset the balance of the various life forms in the ocean in ways that no-one can predict. The only thing we know for certain is that in regions of the ocean where algae blooms are higher, the biodiversity is lower. And the one thing that most of the ideas have in common is that they will encourage the growth of algae. Once again, this is just common sense. When algae grows on stagnant water, it kills virtually all life forms in the water.

So far we have discussed ways in which we can stimulate vegetation and the oceans to capture more of the CO_2 we put into the atmosphere. There is clearly another approach, and that is to capture the gas when it is produced, and then store it somewhere. Since the largest single producer of CO_2 is the power industry, this is the area that has attracted the most attention.

Before we go any further, it is worth reiterating that the objective of the Kyoto Protocol is not to stop all CO_2 emissions, but simply to bring them back to levels that the atmosphere can deal with naturally. This is important, because it means that so long as we capture and store emissions from the main polluters we can satisfy the protocol and, much more significantly, halt global warming.

There is a lot of experience in the USA in reducing emissions of sulfur and nitrous oxides by scrubbing the flue gases with solvents. When it comes to removing CO_2, the same type of technology can be applied; the most likely solvent would be monoethanolamine (MEA). This comes as a liquid, although it can be a solid that is then dissolved in water. When MEA is cold, it can absorb a lot of CO_2, which it then gives up when heated.

The first sign that this was going to be tried seriously came only recently. Royal Dutch/Shell, bP, Chevron, Norsk Hydro, Statoil, Texaco and Suncor announced a joint venture called the CO_2 Capture Project, in which each company would invest $20 million. The objective is to find ways to separate CO_2 at source in power generation and store it. If we remember that CO_2 is a gas, we understand why they would seek this solution. Over the years, these companies have invested a lot of money in gas-to-liquids technology, and there is a wealth of practical experience to draw upon in terms of pipelines and transport as liquid in pressurized containers.

When it comes to storage, the project is looking to inject the CO_2 into geological structures, a procedure that is currently in use at the well head for increasing the oil yield. At the point the project was announced, the cost was estimated to be $5–15/ton of CO_2. The advantage of using oil and gas reservoirs to store CO_2 has the obvious advantage that the oil companies know the geology of the reservoirs already, and by definition they are very large.

We have already talked about the flow of carbon between the various reservoirs. At this point it is worth looking at the amount of carbon stored. The atmosphere currently holds around 745 units of carbon, while the oceans hold something of the order of 40 000 units. So while the steady increase of around three units into the atmosphere may tip the balance, the same amount in the oceans is not really going to be noticed. In fact, to put the size of the ocean into context, it is estimated that the total recoverable fossil fuel reserves in the world amount to about 4000 units. The ocean is the largest carbon storage depot in the world, and there is clearly a lot it can do to help us out.

To be more precise, we should say that the *deep* ocean is the largest store available, for while the surface of the ocean is saturated with carbon, the depths are not. The problem, which we can turn to our advantage, is that it takes a long time for the carbon to move from the surface to the depths. The trick then is to bypass surface absorption, and inject carbon into the deepest parts of the ocean, from where it will take thousands of years to reappear. How we get the CO_2 to the lower depths of the ocean is of course a problem, but nature does provide us with two natural "pumps" that we can take advantage of.

The first is thermohaline circulation. Most movements in the oceans are fast wind-driven currents, but below these are much stronger, slower-circulating movements that result from temperature and salinity differences. The most important of these is the thermohaline current, which plunges to the ocean floor in the North Atlantic, induced by the salty water from the Norwegian current. The current moves south towards Antarctica, from where it spreads to the Pacific and Indian oceans, where it finally resurfaces. The time taken between the sinking in the Atlantic to the resurfacing in the Pacific is at least a few centuries, or possibly a millennium. Smaller but similar currents occur around the Straits of Gibraltar, where a chain of events instigated by evaporation and relative salinity of the water pulls in fresh water from the Atlantic and pushes the escaping water from the Mediterranean down to a deep and slow-moving current.

The second of these natural pumps that can be used relies solely on gravity. Organic matter dies on the surface and sinks slowly to the ocean floor. While most of this plant life is consumed by increasingly large animals, a large enough percentage falls to the floor to be of use.

Only by understanding and exploiting these and the many other smaller currents that exist throughout the world are we going to be able to place the CO_2 at the correct location and depth to ensure that it does not resurface too quickly.

The depth the CO_2 needs to be piped varies from report to report, but appears to be between 1500 and 3000 meters. Obviously, if the CO_2 is put at too shallow a depth it will rise again immediately as a gas. Slightly lower and it will upset the marine life in the area. On the other hand, it costs money to put it at any great depth.

There are all sorts of fascinating chemical facts we could go into at this stage, but we will spare you the details. Here is one interesting fact: only 1% of the CO_2 that goes into the ocean actually remains as CO_2; the rest is converted into other carbon compounds, over 90% of which are stored as bicarbonate ions.

There are three approaches that have been suggested to transfer the CO_2 into the ocean. The first is simply to drop a vertical pipe to about 3000 meters. At these depths, CO_2 is heavier than water and the pressure and temperature would ensure it stays as a liquid. The result is that it would collect together into a pool of liquid CO_2. To do this would require having a floating platform at sea. An alternative to this is to let the CO_2 fall through a pipe attached to a moving ship to a level of 1500 meters. In this way it would dissolve and be dispersed in the water. Finally, it has been suggested that we could use a fixed land-based pipe, which the CO_2 would roll down to a depth of over 1500 meters.

Science and rationality should go hand in hand, but sometimes the laws of physics are broken. At the furthest extremes of environmental science there is no obvious relationship between the two. In this case the extreme is where scientists have decided that rather than deal with liquid CO_2 they would go the extra mile and convert it to a solid. We have included our three favorite proposals in this context.

The first proposal[6] starts with the fact that solid CO_2 is heavier than

[6]   W. Seifritz, 1993. This and the next two examples were brought to our attention by Ben Matthews in his article 'Climate engineering', Scientists for Global Responsibility, November 1996.

water. It is in fact one and half times as dense; if it can be shaped into the form of a torpedo, it can be dropped, like a bomb, into the ocean, where it will travel to the deepest depth and lodge itself within the sediment. Since the CO_2 would reform into an ice-like substance, clathrate hydrate, it would remain locked away for centuries. A lot of research has been done in the area of projectile shapes to ensure that the torpedoes are dispatched efficiently. Like us, you are probably thinking to yourself that you should have thought of that sooner and patented the process. Before you start kicking yourself, there is more to come.

Another concept involves freezing CO_2 into dry ice snowballs. Scientists have calculated that the ideal size for this snowball would be 400 meters in diameter. These snowballs would not be kept cold forever, but would be allowed to slowly release the CO_2 over a very long period of time. The scientists responsible for this proposal assume that if these giant snowballs are allowed to dissolve over an 800-year period, the world would have been given ample time to find a replacement for fossil fuel. In other words, this approach redistributes the emissions from a short period of time over a much longer period, hopefully at a rate that the atmosphere can absorb without causing a problem.

This idea was taken one step further with the idea that the CO_2 could be shipped to Antartica and stored within the ice sheet.[7] One drawback with this is obviously that if global warming melts the ice it will release the CO_2 in a sudden rush, which would cause considerably more damage than we are inflicting upon ourselves already and rapidly accelerate the timetable for climate change.

It is unlikely, and perhaps dangerous to assume, that nature can be coerced to store more carbon; most importantly, it probably represents a false solution. Collecting and storing CO_2 may be possible at source, but it will certainly represent a considerable cost added on to the price of power. A lot of money has already been invested in "carbon sinks", and

[7] Honjou and San, 1995. Also from Ben Matthews, 'Climate engineering'.

energy companies have a lot to lose if they do not come up with a clean procedure for burning fossil fuels. These issues are the most contentious in the debate on the methods of fighting global warming, and top the agenda at the COP-6 meeting.

6

RENEWABLE ENERGY

Before there was Greenpeace, there was Buckminster Fuller. Fuller was uniquely American: unafraid to challenge traditional thinking on design and its place in nature, and an inspiration to an entire generation of environmentalists.[1] In his writings he was the first to describe our world as "Spaceship Earth", and his thoughts on the role of energy in modern life are nothing less than unique. Fuller classified energy as either "capital", "currency", or "short-term savings accounts".[2] He thought of fossil fuels as capital, renewable energies as currency, and biomass as energy stored in short-term savings accounts. By providing a financial structure that quantifies different energy sources, Fuller was stressing the need to save capital, spend currency and keep a short-term savings

---

[1] Fuller's thoughts on the environment were undoubtedly inspired by the time he spent as a professor at Southern Illinois University in Carbondale. Carbondale lies at the center of Little Egypt, a dry and dusty area of the country sandwiched between the Mississippi and Ohio rivers. Coal mining devastated Southern Illinois. During the early 1900s, immigrants from Wales and Ireland flocked to the area to mine coal, and many died from black lung disease later in life.

[2] Tom Stanton, 'Biomass energy: It's not just for breakfast anymore', Michigan Public Service Commission, 1995.

account around for emergencies. Another unique concept of Fuller was to classify biomass as solar energy, for the obvious reason that it requires sunlight to power photosynthesis, which is the basis for all plant life. Wind power was nothing new to Fuller: he grew up in Illinois, where all the farms in the rural part of the state had a windmill to pump water. He did not foresee the development of the commercial windmill, but he did see the obvious benefits of clean hydropower. Fuller is largely ignored by the environmentalists of today, which is a shame. Although many of his ideas and designs proved impractical, his visions on the role of energy in our life made a lot of sense. He would be turning over in his grave now if he saw how these visions have been distorted.

If you happen to have lived in a cave for the past decade, you may not have heard about the unbelievable potential of windmills. Windmills are not only the renewable energy *du jour,* they are now being touted as the new solution to global warming. Politicians love wind power because it is a relatively cheap way of appearing to be green. Environmentalists love wind power for a completely different reason. Windmills singularly represent the all-important link between romanticism and Mother Earth that is the embodiment of the environmental faith.

Unfortunately, once you strip away the mystery and the romance, there is precious little left. They are impractical, uneconomic and environmentally unfriendly. They may produce no greenhouse gases, but the saving represented is so minimal that it barely merits mention. A medium-sized 500-kW windmill operating in perfect conditions saves about as much CO_2 being produced as would be emitted by one semi-trailer truck travelling at 50 mph on an interstate highway.

If you are still under the illusion that there must be something more, something we are not telling you, let us dissect the problem logically. And let us start with the obvious: no wind equals no power. To be more precise, if the wind is not blowing hard enough, the propellers will not turn, and if the wind is howling, the propellers have to be disengaged or the entire structure will come crashing to the ground. These windmills are frail beasts that operate only when the wind is somewhere between 10 and 55 miles per hour,[3] which is, even in the windiest of areas, only a small percentage of the time. On average, they perform as they are designed to do only about one-quarter of the time, which means that they produce only about 25% of the power their makers claim. And they do this in the wildest, windiest and least habitable places on earth.

In any practical sense, it is impossible to store electricity in any quantity. The lifespan of a kilowatt of electricity, from the place of its birth at a local power plant to the point it hits the consumer's socket, is measured in milliseconds. In order for a grid to operate throughout a populated zone, such as the New York metropolitan area, a steady flow of electricity must be produced that just exceeds maximum expected demand. Matching supply and demand is a pretty fine art. Erratic supply, such as that supplied by wind turbines, does the grid no good and therefore is just ignored. Unfortunately, it cannot be totally ignored. To comply with government set targets for the production of "renewable" energy, wind generated electricity has to be purchased. In the real world, where it takes an hour and a half to ramp up a gas-fired turbine and a few days to power up a nuclear plant, planning to meet expected demand requires advance planning. Throwing wind power into the mix, which can vary in output with each gust or lack thereof, will never produce the consistent supply that would be necessary to take fossil-fuelled or nuclear plants offline. Reliability is the main problem with "renewables". The other problem is that even when everything is working at ideal levels, wind power produces virtually no electricity.

[3]   This is based on the Vesta V-47. According to statistics from an implementation in Wisconsin, the start-up wind speed is 9.2 mph, the optimum operating speed is 33.35 mph, and it cuts out at 55 mph.

At the small end of the nuclear spectrum, a generator will produce 1000 MW,[4] while the smallest and most efficient IPPs[5] tend to be of the order of 150 MW. The most advanced and modern wind turbines can generate about 2 MW in power, assuming the wind is blowing in the right direction at exactly the right speed. With a 25% efficiency rate, replacing a small nuclear reactor would take 2000 wind turbines, each of which takes up at least one acre of land, linked together with myriad cables and pylons. Unless we can re-engineer the entire ecosystem to make wind blow at a steady rate all the time, wind power will never provide the world with any substantial benefits.

In the January 2000 edition of *Wind Power Monthly*, it was reported that at the end of 1999 there were around 40 000 turbines in the world, with a maximum output of 12 455 MW. Assuming this is a correct figure, and again assuming a 25% efficiency rate, the total electrical production from all these contraptions would satisfy less than 8% of the UK's needs. Another problem with wind power that is rarely brought up by its advocates has to do with simple mechanics. Although the internal mechanisms are getting better and better, the gear boxes wear out fairly regularly and there is a considerable amount of down time attributable to repairs rather than just a basic lack of wind. Considering all the subsidies the business has received from governments the world over, its lack of success is startling. Wind power would disappear immediately if subsidies were withdrawn. In the UK, wind power costs anything from 116% to 440% of the price of conventionally generated power.[6] In the USA, the figures are much the same, and these costs are passed right along to the con-

[4]   One megawatt (MW) is one million watts; one kilowatt (kW) is one thousand watts.

[5]   Independent power producers. IPPs are smaller producers that are playing an increasing role in the deregulated markets of the USA and the UK. These typically generate electricity by burning gas.

[6]   'The Case Against Windfarms', research report from *Country Guardian*, May 2000.

sumer. Although most consumers will never have their lights powered by the whistling wind, they end up paying for it anyway. Whole areas of the south-eastern USA, which are considered unsuitable for wind power, have to subsidize the installation of turbines throughout the west and east coasts. Considering the disproportionate amounts of subsidies these generators receive, some have even suggested it would be more practical to use the money to bribe truck drivers to stay off the road.

Wind power is still being touted as being "green" solely on the basis that it produces some electrical power without producing greenhouse gases. This is, in theory, true, although very few who have any real concern for the environment think the sort of structures that are being built today are environmentally friendly. Aesthetically, they have been described as either shocking or just bone-jarringly ugly. The structures are nothing like their smaller brethren that line some of the hillsides in southern California. The towers of the Vesta V-47 models in operation in Texas are 275 feet high, with blades more than 100 feet long. The overall height is 375 feet, and they are 200 feet wide. If you are searching for perspective, focus on this: the Statue of Liberty is 301 feet (foundation to torch), and Big Ben is 316 feet tall. Imagine the landscape dominated by 100 such structures, visible at a distance of 20 miles. And here is the crux of the problem: they need wind, so the best places are plains or hill tops, the very places that are considered most naturally beautiful and the most visible from a distance. It's not just the sight of them that bothers most people: they are also inherently unsafe and incredibly noisy. The propellers, which are handmade from Fiberglas, turn at the rate of 180 mph. Simple fatigue can make them splinter or tear off from their axis and hurtle hundreds of feet to the ground. When they become iced, the spinning propeller can throw off chunks weighing one and a half tons over 1000 feet. They also produce a low-frequency noise, similar to the blades of a large helicopter or the sound of a loud party next door when the thumping bass is not only something you hear but feel. There is also the noise from the whirring of the gears, but this problem is solvable and is being addressed. The thudding sound will never go away. It is almost impossible to move an object through the air without creating noise. A hundred of these behemoths thudding all together in unison must be a sound to be heard, perhaps only once though.

It is because of this noise pollution and physical danger that they have to be placed some distance from houses. Unfortunately, that does not help the birds that are regularly cut to pieces in these contraptions. In California, these "green machines" kill in excess of 7000 birds a year, including about 50 golden eagles. Fans would argue that this is the result of bad planning, putting too many together and thus creating a wall that blocks the path of migrating birds. But if we intend to ever use this resource to produce any significant level of power this is going to happen time and time again.

Let's digress for a few moments and pretend we are captains of industry. We have entered a nightmare world of finance where rational thought has been outlawed. Imagine being the chief executive of a major utility and going to an investment bank to ask for a multimillion dollar bond issue to be underwritten for a "special" new power plant. A power plant that would only work, on average, about 25% of the time, and would produce electricity that was three or four times more costly than the price of competitive power. And then imagine explaining that the plant would extend over hundreds of acres, kill thousands of migratory birds each year, blight the landscape, require an expensive installation of miles of power cables and not be located near any major population center.

When we got to the point of explaining that the lifespan of the plant would he half that of a normal generator, for most of us the shear humiliation of it would be too much to bear. But this is a romantic world where windmills represent ideals, and not only would we be taken seriously, but the chances are the investment bankers would be falling all over us to fill our glasses with champagne and light our cigars.

If we put ourselves in the place of a politician, who is naturally much more worried about the next term in office than global warming, think of how much we would love environmentalists. They not only represent a sizeable portion of the electorate, but they bring with them an incredibly cheap solution to a very expensive problem. It does not matter that the solution is blatantly false: by virtue of their endorsement, the solution is validated. All we have to do is force the utilities to make consumers subsidize the cost of wind power, and we can pretend that such a thing like renewable energy actually exists and that we are doing something about global warming. But, most importantly, if the taxpayers are already footing the bill for it all without their knowledge, we do not have to present a real solution that involves higher taxes. Because if we presented a program that provoked a real debate about the merits of wind power, we would be laughed out of office.

The next European target for windmills on a wide scale is Ireland. Having failed in Denmark and Britain, the developers are now armed with EU subsidies and tax breaks and are targeting 40 sights in the country. Not only would the installation of wind farms destroy the country's natural beauty, it would also devastate the tourist trade. Given the amount of local opposition it is unlikely that many proposals will be accepted. The problem the locals face, though, is complicated by the $1.2 million in subsidies each windmill earns from the EU for its 20-year lifespan.[7] This gives the developers a tremendous amount of buying power when they are facing stiff local political opposition.

A rational argument about the merits of wind power would last all of about 30 seconds. It is not practical, it is not economic and it is not even environmentally friendly. The next time a politician turns misty eyed

---

[7]   Dan Danaher, 'Wind farm to blow away tourists', *The Clare Champion*, 11 August 2000, p. 1.

and mentions the benefits of renewable energy, listen hard. If you detect the slightest glint in his eye and a barely concealed grin, he might just have the same sense of humor as you.

Many city dwellers long for the countryside, but when they get there find that it is not the romantic, idealized place they had dreamed of. Windmills are similarly idealized by people who do not have to live near them and have probably never seen or heard one.

Biomass is a classic example of a good idea gone horribly wrong. In its original form, biomass works and does produce relatively clean power by simply utilizing what we throw away. And the easiest example of biomass is wood chips. When trees are harvested for wood and paper production, large amounts are left over. If you take into account the tops, branches, roots, bark and leaves, up to 75% is left unused. Why not burn this to produce heat?

Another inspiration for biomass must have been the compost heap: when organic matter decays, it emits gases. One of these gases is CO_2, but others include combustible gases such as methane.[8] The theory behind biomass in its good form is to build facilities to process organic matter, in much the same way as they process oil, and to capture the gases and other products that are emitted. In this way we can create biogas (very similar to natural gas), biodiesel and other products. It is a good theory because the raw material is free, and the CO_2 that we create would have been emitted by the decaying material anyway, and we are simply taking advantage of it to generate heat. The process of creating biomass-generated fuel that we have described is just the good part, though. It all starts going horribly wrong when the genetic engineers get involved.

Thanks to the wonders of gene splicing we are now able to grow trees at the rate of over 10 feet a year. Although it has yet to be tried on any

---

[8]   Actually, when you think about it, all natural gas is derived from biomass. Natural gas is just methane, which comes from rotting organic matter, the liquid part of which is crude oil.

large scale, the next generation of biomass is all about planting trees with the express purpose of cutting them down for fuel. In a world in which we need all available quality land for agricultural production, the thought of growing forests and burning them down for electricity appears to be a step too far. Environmentalists are also trying to push the concept of "fuel crops", which would be grown specifically to burn for electrical production. This is nothing new, and is a common practice in Mauritius where farmers burn the waste from sugar cane to generate electricity. The idea of developing specific crops for this purpose, without any food value, seems like a massive misuse of good land when half the world cannot afford food.

The original concept of biomass fuel is to consume waste. Theoretically it is an excellent idea, because if waste cannot be recycled it might as well be burned for heat. Practically, though, it becomes exceedingly important to sort the waste and exclude hazardous materials from the process, otherwise burning trash for fuel becomes deadly. Getting people to go through the process of individually sorting out every piece of rubbish they throw away is not something that is going to be done overnight. Burning waste also produces particulate pollution, which causes severe health problems. Where it has been tried, for example in Lisbon, the public reaction has been so great that the process had to be called to a halt.

The fact of the matter is we are already producing biomass fuel in great quantities, but we are simply not using it. Landfills in New Jersey and Staten Island that have been covered and turned into green areas are literally bombs waiting to go off. Methane has to be vented from the surface to prevent the real risk of explosion. To develop methods to commercially store the methane from landfills does not entail a major engineering feat, and to redesign future rubbish dumps so they can be covered and emit natural gas in a manner that makes storage easy is not nearly as difficult as splitting the atom. Even if we do this, though, we would simply not produce sufficient quantities to make biomass commercially viable. In this case, though, not to do it would be a worse alternative.

If solar power really worked, people would be knocking on your door to sell you panels, just like they did with aluminum siding in the 1960s. If it really made commercial sense, why is it not everywhere? There is no evil conspiracy to keep it away from you. Why is it not common in the suburbs of Boston or Edinburgh? Smart people live in both cities, and if they could save heaps on their electrical bills by putting up solar panels on their roofs, they would certainly be doing it.

To say solar power does not work is not fair. It does work, sometimes. It works in the right places, during the daytime, and when the sun shines. Beware of the people that tell you it works even with cloud cover. A six-cylinder car engine "works" on two cylinders, but it is not going to get you very far. Solar power is the stuff of romantic books and fairy tales. We dream of harnessing the natural heat of the sun so that all God's children can play and live happily ever after, and we can stop worrying about those relentless bills from the utility companies. Unfortunately, what with the fact that it is dark half the time, and clouds reduce and scatter the power of the sun, it is very inefficient. In fact, it is operational on average for only 15% of the time. It works extremely well in stationary orbit 100 miles above the earth on the new space station, but if you are counting on solar to run your vacuum cleaner, and it's a rainy day in Georgia, then you are in for a mild shock.

When we say that solar operates only 15% of the time, we are being more than a bit disingenuous. Solar works in some places pretty well. In Cyprus and Israel, for example, solar panels are an accepted feature of the landscape. They are not powering factories, but they are heating hot water for home use. They are saving individuals money on fuel bills and, as they reduce some demand on the grid, they are doing their bit to save the world from global warming. Taking solar power further than just heating water is a different matter. There are two ways that solar power can be used to generate electricity: either we can use the heat in the same way as we do that of coal, or we can use photovoltaic cells. Unfortunately photovoltaic cells are very expensive, but there are examples of using the heat.

The Central Tower Power Plant has 1800 parabolic mirrors, which are computer controlled so that the sun's rays are continually refocused to the top of the tower. This then heats up a liquid and this heat is transferred to create steam, which then turns the turbine to generate electrical power. Similar large-scale projects using mirrors to refocus the sun in this way are in place. All of these facilities[9] are in California. They may yet prove to be economically viable, but they require continuous sunlight to work at full efficiencies. They do not provide a backbone of power upon which to base a grid.

If we make massive leaps in technology, the amount of power we can generate from the sun will always be minuscule. On a sunny day in Australia it is possible to capture up to 1 kW of power per square meter of solar panels, if they are placed at the right angle to the sun. Given that an average person living in a developed country uses around 900 kW of electricity throughout the day,[10] each person would need a solar panel about 900 square meters in size to satisfy his or her power needs. If you happen to live in a northern climate, the size of the panel would have to increase significantly, and it would have to work in the dark. It would be essential that it worked during the most bitter winter blizzard or on the coldest night, as this is when power demands peak.

Some people just end up at the right place at the right time, and others (like us) have to pay for power. The Ring of Fire is the place where nature has decided to do her own part to heat up the atmosphere. For those

[9] That we know of.
[10] Direct and indirect consumption.

lucky enough to live on this geological fault line, power exists just below the ground and all it takes is a few smart people and a couple of generators to power up the electricity grid. The one problem with the Ring of Fire is that it is a bubbling caldron of greenhouse gases, and it smells like some terrible vision of hell. Geothermal energy uses the natural heat in the earth. This is the energy that publicly manifests itself in the form of geysers and volcanoes. To use this heat means either directly leveraging off these geysers and volcanoes or drilling through the earth's surface to find the heat.

It is not going to surprise you to learn that the areas of the world where geothermal energy is used in any significant way are the same regions that are associated with volcanoes. These places include California, which has abundant geothermal energy. European locations include Italy and Iceland. In addition it can be found in other parts of the west coast of the USA, Central and South America, the Philippines and New Zealand.

Most of the installations that are in place now are designed to generate electrical power. The concept is exceedingly simple. Underground reservoirs of steam and boiling water are brought to the surface to turn turbines, after which the water is returned underground. The world currently produces around 6000 MW of power by this means, and the figure is growing each year. The largest facility in operation is The Geysers in California, which produces around 1500 MW. In terms of power production, this exceeds most large nuclear reactors. More importantly, it is free and it is constant. This means that it can actually run as a base load source of power.

In addition to this power production, there is a lot of low-level heat available. Even low-level heat is tremendously valuable. Although the water may not be hot enough to turn a turbine, heating it to that point requires very little additional power. It can also be used to heat homes and industrial complexes directly.

It is clear that this is a source of energy that makes sense in a few parts of the world. But for most of us it is likely to remain a pipe dream: a wonderful fantasy of being able to put a pipe in the back garden and tap into the heat in the earth's core and enjoying free natural continuous energy. If technology is developed and this possibility becomes available, we could shut down every power station in the world. It has been estimated that the heat in the top five miles of the earth's crust contains about 50 000 times the amount of energy stored in known oil and gas reserves.

Everybody loves a beaver. They are such industrious creatures and, just like us, love chopping down trees, building dams and fouling up the environment. Hydroelectric power was once the favorite of the environmentalists, until they met up and fell in love with the windmill. Although the beaver may still hold a special place in their hearts, the human dam builders are now not so loved.

In some cases, cheap electricity is just not worth it. A good rule of thumb to follow when analyzing any hydro project is that if it is big and in a developing country, it is all about producing cheap power for the wealthy urban classes and creating hell on earth for the rural poor. China is an excellent case in point. In order to power up the industrial corridor, the entire landscape is being changed and a few million peasants who are living in the wrong place are being "resettled". A big hydro project produces an ecological and human disaster that makes Chernobyl look like the good old days.

Hydropower is more an ethical issue than an energy issue. It is a moral trade-off between meeting the power needs for a future generation as opposed to destroying the lives of millions, ruining a natural habitat and ending a way of life that can never be brought back into existence again. The Three Gorges Dam[11] project will displace any number of people, but it will also flood 1300 archaeological sights, destroy the natural environment for endangered species of animals and rare plants, and trap more

[11] The world's biggest dam, being built in China.

than 50 types of pollutants from mines, cities and factories.[12] The argument constantly posed to discourage further investment in nuclear power is that we are creating a problem that will extend into future generations. This is perfectly reasonable, but hydropower ends current generations of living things forever, negating any need to worry about the future. The risks of hydro are never discussed fully. A dam should not inspire ultimate confidence, particularly one sitting right on the Ring of Fire. We are aware of the risks associated with nuclear power and earthquakes, but we dismiss the risks of hydropower and cataclysmic events. In 1963, the Vaiont Dam in Italy split open sending a tidal wave 328 feet high down a valley and through many villages. The result was a tremendous loss of life and destruction of property. The Three Gorges Dam will create a reservoir 370 miles long. If this dam ever gave way the results would be devastating.

If we concentrate on where the money is really going, it is all being spent on massive hydroelectric projects in India and China. China is intending to install an additional 100 GWh of power by the year 2010. This would provide the country with 30% of its expected power needs, and simultaneously reduce flooding along the Yangtze river. Annual floods along the river basin kill thousands of people and destroy hundreds of houses. But flooding also makes the land rich and improves crop yields naturally. The world's largest hydroelectric project to date, the Three Gorges Dam project, will produce 18.2 GWh of power. The estimated cost is in the range of $25 billion. Germany and Canada have been instrumental in providing finance for the project, and General Electric and Siemens are providing technical support.[13] China is doing much to bring rural areas on to the grid and to supply electricity to all its citizens. The

[12] 'Hydroelectricity and other renewable sources', *International Energy Outlook 1999*, published by the EIA.
[13] 'Hydroelectricity and other renewable sources', *International Energy Outlook 1999*, published by the EIA.

Three Gorges Dam project will go some way to meeting the needs of the country, but it will not do much for the one million plus peasants that are being forcefully displaced.

The environmentalists did have a brief fling with the mini-hydro. These were small dams meant to produce 5–15 MW of power, which is just enough power to bake a few loaves of bread. Of course, they ignored the fact that a dam is a dam, and, just like a small drug problem is still a drug problem, even a small dam messes up the environment. Small hydro is not efficient, construction costs are too high to recoup expenses, and the technical expertise required to run a small hydro project outweighs the value of the power it produces.

At least windmills work some of the time. If you put your money on ocean power being your electricity provider for the future you are far braver than we are. The three potential sources of power to be derived from the ocean come from wave power, tidal power and the theoretical possibility of exploiting the temperature difference between the surface of the ocean and the colder depths. Each one is in fact more ill conceived than the other.

Wave energy is supposed to derive from the kinetic movement of the ocean's mass. There are a couple of ways that are being investigated to capture this energy and to turn it into useful power. One involves sticking turbines near the shore, which would spin when a wave rushes through the chamber. The other involves sticking a barrage in front of oncoming waves, which powers pistons at each end. Both systems have been tested and neither works.

Another theoretical way to capture the power of the oceans is to dam up harbors at high tide, and to utilize gravity to power hydroelectric turbines. This is actually not so far fetched, but it would only work at higher latitudes where tide heights are considerable. The costs would be enormous and the turbine would work in the same way as a blender, liquefying all sea life that felt the irresistible pull of gravity and current.

Ocean thermal energy conversion (OTEC) is the most bizarre of all the proposed renewable energies. In essence, OTEC is all about exploiting the temperature difference between various layers of the ocean to produce electricity. There is nothing wrong with the theory; the problem comes down to the location. For this to work requires a big difference in temperatures, which only occurs in the deep ocean. This means the "power plant" has to be on board a ship well out to sea. Until we can figure out how to put pylons on the surface of the ocean, delivering the power generated from this source to a populated area becomes fairly problematic.

With few exceptions, renewable energy is a pipe dream. It is neither green nor reliable. In addition, most of it is low-output and expensive. There is absolutely no way, even in combination, that it can ever replace fossil fuels. While it may help a little in alleviating the problem of global warming, it is certainly not the answer. Certain renewables deserve further investment, such as geothermal and biomass, but they are not sources of energy that will make a dent in the problem that we are currently facing, nor will they replace the fuels that are causing the problem of global warming.

Matt Ridley, an English scientist and social commentator, summed it up better than we could when he wrote:

> Wind is the most promising of all alternative energies, yet it is catastrophic for the landscape and an economic nonsense. Wind farms generate minuscule amounts of electricity in the wrong place at the wrong time. And they ruin the landscape. And they chop up eagles. To replace oil and gas in the economy we would need to cover our hills with windmills, dam our rivers for hydro power, ruin our estuaries with tidal barrages, put solar panels everywhere – and still

we would need nuclear power for most of the demand. If we were in that situation, and discovered oil and gas for the first time, imagine what a godsend they would seem. Imagine the fury with which the green lobby would demand the removal of dams and windmills and their replacement by gas turbines.[14]

[14] Matt Ridley, 'Beyond petroleum lies big trouble', *Daily Telegraph*, 8 August 2000, p. 18.

7

NUCLEAR ENERGY

When was the last time you read something positive about nuclear power in the newspaper? Stumped? It would be interesting to know who in the nuclear power industry chooses the PR firms that represent them, and it would be even more interesting to know what these PR firms do with their time. There are some negative things to say about nuclear energy, but there are also a lot of positive things; but in the same way that a double homicide sells the newspapers, it is the bad news that gets the press. If the public is going to embrace nuclear power, the bad press has to be addressed and put into perspective first.

When we think about nuclear power, we tend to think of the bad things, and it is not long before the name "Chernobyl" comes to mind. Although this incident occurred a decade and a half ago, the experience lingers with us. The truth is that Chernobyl was a huge, poorly designed reactor that lacked even the most basic safety technology. The explosion at Chernobyl was, ironically, the result of a safety drill gone wrong. The operators were attempting to determine how long the turbines would continue to spin in the event of a power outage. The tests were done at the lowest possible power settings, and this is where the design fault of the reactor manifested itself. During the process of the test, the automatic shut-down procedures were disabled. At some point in the process, the operator moved to shut down the reactor entirely and the trouble started: power surged dramatically, rupturing the fuel elements. The steam in the reactor built up, blowing the cover plate off. Fission products were thrown into the atmosphere. A second explosion threw out fuel and allowed oxygen to rush in to fuel a fire. The graphite moderators caught fire and burned for nine days. This caused the greatest release of radiation into the atmosphere.[1] The accident killed 31 people, and contaminated an area around the plant. The most lasting affect has been an increase in thyroid cancer among children in the area, although this is usually treatable and seldom results in fatality.[2]

The incident at Chernobyl was about as bad as any nuclear incident could get. It led to a complete overhaul of all Soviet style reactors, and the decommissioning of the most seriously flawed facilities. Chernobyl still operates its other two reactors, and 6000 people still work at the plant every day, including a group that work inside the damaged reactor. Radiation levels within the facility are now within acceptable bounds.

The incident at Chernobyl was a PR nightmare for the nuclear industry, as it galvanized support for the anti-nuclear lobby. To compare the incident at Chernobyl with the biggest US incident is like comparing night and day. Three Mile Island is a large nuclear facility in Pennsylvania. On Wednesday, 28 March 1979, a series of control failures occurred at the plant, instigated by the failure of a valve that was an essential control mechanism in the cooling process. The incident resulted in a slight release of radiation into the atmosphere and exposed some safety and instrumentation problems within the plant. The problem was greatly

---

[1]   'Chornobyl [Chernobyl] and Soviet Reactors', *Nuclear Issues Briefing Paper 22*, UIC, March 2000.

[2]   The immediate distribution of potassium iodide tablets could have prevented most of the thyroid cancer cases. The UK has stockpiled the drug at all public health facilities as a precaution against any sort of serious nuclear incident.

exaggerated by the press, which led to panic among the civilian population in the area. Since 1985, the plant has operated perfectly without
one significant incident.

The most recent accident occurred in September 1999, at Tokaimura,
Japan. Again, this was a result of lack of experience, but this one is easy to
explain. Three workers poured 16 kg of uranium into a settling tank designed to contain 2.5 kg. The real problem was that the uranium should
have been added gradually via a filtration unit, instead of being poured
from a steel bucket. The result was that they started a self-sustaining
chain reaction. Tokaimura is a privately owned processing plant rather
than a nuclear reactor.

In the last 20 years, there have been three nuclear accidents in the
world. Of these, only Chernobyl was considered to be a major accident,[3]
and was the "result of a flawed reactor design that was operated with
inadequately trained personnel and without proper regard for safety."[4]
The other two, Three Mile Island and Tokaimura, both resulted primarily
from lack of training, and both were contained and controlled extremely
quickly.[5]

Chernobyl was a nightmare not just for Chernobyl, but also for the
nuclear industry globally. A top executive in the French nuclear industry
would not smirk and feel a smug satisfaction that he had gained a competitive advantage because the Soviet Union had shown they were in-
capable of running a nuclear plant. Any nuclear accident dents the image
of the whole industry. Not only did the world rush to the aid of the Soviet
Union directly after the incident, but the process is still ongoing. Since

[3] The official scale that measures the seriousness of a nuclear event is the
International Nuclear Events Scale (INES). The scale goes from 0 to 7, where
0 is a deviation, 1–3 are classed as incidents, and 4–7 are accidents. On this
scale Chernobyl was a 7.
[4] 'Chornobyl [Chernobyl] and Soviet Reactors', *Nuclear Issues Briefing Paper 22*,
UIC, March 2000.
[5] On the INES scale, these were both deemed to be level 5.

the accident, over 1000 scientists from the former Soviet Union have visited western nuclear plants, and similar visits have been made by western scientists to the former Soviet Union. In 1989, the industry set up the World Association of Nuclear Operators, drawing together representatives of nuclear plants from more than 30 countries. There have been a number of twinning arrangements between nuclear scientists in the east and the west. This is one of the few industries where everyone pulls together. There is no competitive advantage to having the only safe reactor in town. The result has been that safety procedures have developed immeasurably. To date, we have 9400 nuclear years behind us, and the track record, if we want to be open minded and fair about things, is excellent.

The risk of radiation exposure is what most people find most terrifying about nuclear power, although most of us are exposed to it, or use it, every day of our lives. Much of the food we eat has been bombarded with radioactive particles in order to "purify" it and to increase its shelf life. Irradiation is used, like freezing and heating, to destroy insects and bacteria. The safety of this procedure has been confirmed by the US Food and Drug Administration, independent scientific committees in the UK, Sweden and other countries, and the World Health Organization, amongst others.

Radiation is also used extensively in medicine to diagnose and treat various diseases, including cancer, and for sterilizing instruments. In the USA alone there are over 28 000 doctors whose specialities rely on radiation.[6] Virtually every US hospital has some form of nuclear medical unit, which in total perform more than 10 million nuclear-based operations every year. And of the Nobel Prizes given in the areas of medicine and physiology from 1975 to 1989, 10 were based on research using radioactive materials.

Radioactive material is also used extensively in industry since it emits

[6]   These facts are from the Nuclear Energy Institute.

signals that can be monitored. So it is used in pipes to find leaks, exploration to generate maps, and in car and jet engines to expose weaknesses. Radiation is also, of course, a natural part of living on planet earth. A nuclear incident is a scary thing, but a world without nuclear power is a much scarier place.

The insidious dangers posed by the uncontrolled burning of fossil fuels are no longer news, and in the same way as reports on the dangers of cigarette smoking, these stories are no longer going to sell newspapers. The dramatic deaths of the fire fighters in Chernobyl makes much better reading than writing about the three million people who die each year due to air pollution, simply because they happen much less often. Nuclear reactors produce the least amount of waste material when compared with any other reliable source of energy. The waste is not diffused into the atmosphere and, if stored properly, does not pose any danger to mankind.

Many of us have some idea of how a nuclear reactor works, but have little interest in the real mechanics. Quite simply, starting a chain reaction is like setting light to a tree. If the tree is a long way from other trees it will burn out. The closer it is to other trees, the higher the danger that another one will catch fire, and the process will spread from tree to tree. There is obviously a certain density, or distance between the trees, for this chain reaction to occur. At the extreme, if the trees were densely packed, the fire would rapidly leap from one to the other, very quickly creating an uncontrollable inferno. A nuclear reactor works in the same way. At the core is uranium, which is a naturally occurring element. The interesting thing is that uranium exists in two forms, only one of which is fissionable;[7] it is the fissionable variety that decays and creates heat. In

---

[7] Fission is the act of decaying, which is what we want. When uranium decays, it gives off heat. For those of you who need to know, the two isotopes are U-235 (the fissionable one) and U-238. The number indicates the number of particles in the nucleus.

nature, only 0.7% of the uranium we come across is fissionable, which is equivalent to having trees placed very far apart. To get to the critical density so that the fire leaps from one tree to the next, the level of fissionable uranium has to be around 4%. At this level, once we have set light to one tree, the chain reaction keeps it going. But because we are only around the critical density, we can slow it down using control rods that effectively create firewalls within the core of the reactor. The obvious question is, what is the difference between this type of reaction and that used in a nuclear bomb? The difference is that the nuclear bomb is equivalent to the uncontrollable inferno in the forest. The density of the fissionable uranium is taken from 0.7% not to 4% but to 90%. At this level, the material literally explodes. In a reactor, the chain reaction is slow and controlled; in a bomb, it is violent and uncontrollable. A reactor does not produce a bomb.

There are still a lot of people around who are concerned that the ability to build a nuclear reactor obviously translates into the ability to produce an atomic weapon. The shear fear of nuclear proliferation was at the basis for the ratification of the Nuclear Non Proliferation Treaty. The implementation of the treaty is overseen by the International Atomic Energy Agency (IAEA), who have sweeping powers to ensure that countries are in compliance. The treaty has been extraordinarily successful, because the world is pulling together to make it work, in much the same way as they are working together to increase the safety of nuclear reactors.

As a matter of interest, decommissioned nuclear weapons are now being used to provide fuel for the reactors, although this requires a lot of "watering down" of the enriched uranium from the 90% levels to 4%.

One thing the environmental lobby can use to scare the world is the perceived threat posed by nuclear waste. The reality is that the waste is not the crawling green slime that science fiction films would have you believe, and the volume is incredibly low.

Nuclear fuel comes in the form of solid ceramic pellets about the size of a fingertip; it looks the same before and after it is used. This small pellet contains the same amount of energy as a railroad car full of coal, or 17 000 cubic feet of natural gas. As the enriched uranium is used, the active element is "burnt"; once it falls below a certain percentage, the fuel effectively stops working. When the fuel is removed from the reactor, only 3% of it is actually waste; the other 97% can be recycled, as it is in Europe. One of the ways that this spent fuel is dealt with is called vitrification, which in simple terms means that it is embedded in molten glass. The glass is then put into stainless steel containers, which are welded shut. To provide some sense of the quantity of waste produced, a tennis ball-sized piece of this vitrified glass would contain the waste produced in supplying power to one person for their entire lifetime.

For historical reasons, the USA does not recycle nuclear waste. When most of the US nuclear plants were built, they had intended to reprocess the spent fuel. The decision not to came in 1979, when President Carter banned the process as a way of addressing public concerns about the proliferation of nuclear weapons. The result is that the volume of waste is higher, but it is less toxic. Even though it is not recycled, and bearing in mind that the USA gets around 20% of its energy from nuclear reactors, the total amount of nuclear waste produced in the USA to date in over 40 years of use would cover a baseball pitch to a depth of five yards.[8]

When we compare this volume of waste with 20 billion tons of CO_2 emitted into the atmosphere each year, the volume begins to become at least psychologically manageable. The average reactor creates about 10 cubic meters of waste a year, compared with four million tons of CO_2 emitted from a typical coal-fired generator. Although nuclear waste is a long-term issue, if we buy the concept of global warming, CO_2 is a waste that is in fact much more dangerous over both the short and long term. Managing nuclear waste is a minor problem compared with the effects

[8]   Data from the Nuclear Energy Institute, 2000.

that global warming will have on the world. The waste material created to generate the power everyone uses and propel the cars we drive has already started destroying the planet we live on. Nuclear power does produce waste, but unlike the waste from fossil fuel that immediately gets into the atmosphere, creating acid rain and global warming, at least nuclear waste is contained.

Simply because the size of all the nuclear waste the world has generated to date is so small, the management of this waste is not a significant problem. Until long-term solutions are found, the waste sits in sealed containers above ground. Eventually, sites will be certified that are deep in the ground and protected by layers of salt and clay. If leakage were to eventually occur, the radioactivity would be dissipated and would pose no risk to mankind. The fact that the world recognizes the danger of nuclear waste assures us that a solution will be found to deal with the problem. As the world does not recognize the risk of fossil fuel waste, the danger is simply ignored.

Eskom is a South African power company. Its research staff have developed a cheap and safe "pocket" nuclear reactor that can be set up in months for the fraction of the cost of a major nuclear facility. Eskom, which already operates numerous coal-fired power stations, decided to look into nuclear energy because of the growing problem with particulate pollution. Its criteria were that the power station should be economically competitive against its existing coal-fired power stations, could be sited anywhere, and would be accepted by the public.

The reactor they designed is unique, and has been named the pebble bed modular reactor (PBMR). The name "pebble" comes from the fact that the fuel comes in spherical balls, much the same size as a tennis ball. The reactors are referred to as "modular" simply because each small 110-MW reactor can be linked to others to increase capacity as needed. Besides price and convenience, what makes them truly unique is that their design makes it virtually impossible for the reactor core to melt down. Because of this, the skill levels required to operate the reactor are much lower than those required to operate a major nuclear facility. Each reactor measures 27 × 53 meters, and is 47 meters high, half of which is below ground. Four reactors could fit inside a football field, and the safety exclusion zone around them is only 400 meters, as opposed to 10 miles for a normal reactor.

The PBMRs will be prebuilt and shipped in pieces to their destinations. They are the first factory-produced reactors and, as the economies of scale work in their favor, they will be as economically competitive as virtually any other type of electrical generator. To understand how the PBMR works and what makes it safe takes a few moments, but we warn you, it is a little difficult to make this part interesting.

First of all, this is not a totally unique design but a modification of existing technologies. The PBMR is a high temperature gas cooled reactor (HTR), as opposed to a pressurized water reactor (PWR). An HTR uses helium (an inert gas) as opposed to water to cool the reactor. Helium does not corrode the pipes, and virtually negates the risk of leakage. Graphite is used in PBMRs as the moderator. The type of moderator used in a reactor has a direct bearing on its inherent safety, and graphite is considered the safest and most efficient of all. Instead of fuel rods, the PBMR uses baseball-sized balls of graphite embedded with ceramic pellets, which contain enriched uranium. By using helium gas as a coolant, combined with graphite- and ceramic-encased fuel, the reactor can work at much greater efficiencies and higher temperatures than a normal PWR. A PBMR operates at temperatures of 750 °C, as opposed to 300 °C for a PWR. As a result, efficiency is about 18% higher in a PBMR.[9]

One of the other advantages with this design is that the reactor does

[9] Steve Thomas, *PBMRs in South Africa: Arguments on the construction of pebble bed modular reactors in South Africa*, SPRU Energy Research, Sussex University, February 1999.

not need to be closed down for refuelling, unlike conventional reactors. Instead, the "pebbles" are continuously taken out and measured to determine if there is enough fissionable material left. They are not replaced all at once, but continuously as they wear out.

The type of fuel that the PBMR uses allays all fears of nuclear proliferation, simply because there is virtually no opportunity to enrich it further to make it into bomb-grade plutonium. The waste material produced by the plant is a fraction of that produced by normal reactors, and the reactor can refuel online, negating the need for an annual shutdown of the facility. The PBMR in its simplest state is an ideal power source for small cities. South Africa sees this reactor as the final solution to wean itself off coal, which is responsible for significant amounts of acid rain falling downwind from plants. South Africa has one of the highest concentrations of acid rain in the world, and the effect has been catastrophic to native plants and trees.

As opposed to other nuclear facilities, the PBMR displays "passive safety", which means that in the event of a fault, the reactor simply comes to a standstill and dissipates heat without the possibility of core failure. The nature of its design makes it easier to operate than a coal-fired generating plant, and can be operated by a team of 10 technicians on revolving shifts. It is estimated that a PBMR can generate electricity at a cost of less than 1.5 cents per kilowatt hour. The estimated cost of building a PBMR reactor is about $55 million, making these reactors cheaper to build, operate and run than even coal-generated plants.

The environmental lobby has examined the advantages of PBMRs and has decided to protest against both Eskom and the PBMR. Given the apparent advantages of the PBMR, it is not clear why they are protesting. The fact is that the PBMR is a massive leap forward in nuclear technology, and looks to be able to produce power on a very cheap scale; once the cost of carbon is factored into the equation, the economics of the PBMR become irresistible. A normal PBMR reactor that produces

100 MW of power would save up to 640 000 tons of CO_2 a year. If these savings are converted into carbon credits, the value amounts to $6–$18 million a year, or at least $240 million during the lifetime of the facility. Assuming there will be a value for CO_2, the PBMR can be self-financing or built virtually for free.

The latest convert to this reactor is British Nuclear Fuels, Ltd (BNFL), which, in June 2000, made a significant investment in what it referred to as a "project to develop what is expected to be the safest, cleanest and most cost-efficient nuclear power source option for the future [the PBMR]."

Living in a polluted city or a polluted world affects human health to a much greater extent than any threat posed by nuclear waste. We know how many people died as a direct result of Chernobyl, but when we compare that figure against the millions of deaths caused by simple pollution the problem pales in significance.

Enter into a different scenario and imagine that you are a parent in rural Kentucky and your 18-year-old son wants to drop out of school and start work. If there were two jobs advertised in the newspaper, one as a coal miner in a deep pit mine or one as a technician in a nuclear power plant, which job would you want your son to take? Although nuclear energy conjures up images of Chernobyl, Three Mile Island, and the panicked looks of Jack Lemmon and Jane Fonda in *The China Syndrome*, a career at a nuclear plant sure sounds better than dying of black lung disease. Nuclear energy will never have a warm and fuzzy image. It is all about releasing the power of the atom, and when we think about that, the first thing that comes to mind is a mushroom cloud. To move beyond these exaggerated nightmares and face reality, we have to accept that nuclear power does exist and it does work. If we want to expand its usefulness, it is the job of all of us to make that happen.

Right now there are only three viable sources of large-scale energy production in the world: fossil fuels, nuclear and hydro. Even if we like hydro, it cannot satisfy any more than a small percentage of the world's demand, and we are forced into making a choice between burning fossil fuels and using nuclear energy. Electricity generated by normal gas turbines produces over one kilogram of CO_2 per kilowatt hour, while nuclear power releases virtually no CO_2.[10] This is a powerful argument in favor of using nuclear power as a primary solution to the problem of climate change, although the opponents of this argument are beyond listening to reason. The most vocal opponent to the inclusion of nuclear within the Kyoto Protocol is Greenpeace. They are campaigning strongly against the inclusion of nuclear as a CDM vehicle. In a classic case of shooting themselves in the foot to prove their case, the organization recently released a statement in which an example of the CDM mechanism was used to demonstrate how nuclear energy could be used to eliminate the problem of global warming. According to Greenpeace:

> A 700 MW coal fired power station emits about 4.5 million tons of CO_2 a year. If a nuclear reactor was built instead, it could be claimed that it offsets this amount of CO_2. Estimates of the value of CO_2 vary, but for a CDM project an amount of approximately $10–30 a ton is likely. Thus the carbon offset by this nuclear reactor over a ten year period would be valued at $450 million and $1.35 billion (less if future credits are discounted).

What the statement failed to point out is that the nuclear power plant would save over 45 million tons of CO_2 from being released into the environment during the course of 10 years. As most nuclear facilities have a lifespan of over 40 years, the savings in terms of CO_2 would amount to over 180 million tons. Greenpeace is also concerned about China, the second biggest emitter of CO_2 in the world, and their plans to push for nuclear to be included in the CDM mechanism. Greenpeace

[10] *Vattenfall's Life-Cycle Studies of Electricity Generation*, Vattendall Energisystem AB and Explicare, January 1997.

states, "If, for example, Canada were to secure another contract to build two 700 MW reactors in China it could potentially claim 9 million tons of carbon reduction credits per annum – equivalent to approximately 6% of its 1998 carbon dioxide emissions."

Greenpeace goes on to state, "Ultimately, the only way to make the CDM an effective vehicle for clean development and global climate protection is to restrict CDM projects to renewable energy technologies." They are actively pushing for a list of "positive" technologies to be made part of the CDM rules. Not only does Greenpeace want to phase out nuclear power, but it would like to phase out all gas generators as well.[11] In so doing they would deprive most of the developed world of electricity, leaving only those types of generators online that produce the highest levels of CO_2. As we saw in the chapter on renewable energy, there is little there that will be much use to India, for example. Are they really going to replace smoking chimney stacks with burning biomass?

It is tempting to think that the environmentalists are feeling more than a little threatened. After all, if nuclear energy is deemed allowable under the Kyoto Protocol it will undoubtedly be used. And the more it is used, the more people will start to see the positive side of it, and before we know it the fear will have gone. Once the fear goes, the battle will have been lost.

We said earlier that nuclear energy would undoubtedly be used. The reason is simple: economics. By creating a value for CO_2, nuclear energy instantly becomes the cheapest option. It will cost up to $30 a ton for CO_2; for a normal gas turbine electricity generator this equates to an additional three cents on the cost of each kilowatt hour, much more for a coal-fired plant. Nuclear power has traditionally been more expensive, but with the implementation of the "carbon tax", it becomes the cheapest power. Wood McKenzie rightly points out that, "The value of carbon

---

[11] Robert L Bradley Jr, 'Policy analysis: renewable energy: not green, not cheap', *Cato Policy Analysis*, The Cato Institute, 27 August 1997, p. 7.

permits will feed directly into generator fuel input prices and thus into generated output unit prices – for fossil fuels only. The higher the value of carbon, the more of a relative price advantage will be conferred on non-fossil fuel power such as renewables, hydro and nuclear."[12] The firm goes on to state, "Premature closure of the largest proven and commercial non-fossil energy source in existence in Europe today will become increasingly unattractive, as and when the reality of Kyoto-driven carbon trading approaches."

This is why Greenpeace and other environmental campaigners do not want nuclear energy included in CDM projects. They are already competitively priced against fossil fuels, so if fossil fuels are taxed, and nuclear energy is allowed to fill the gap, it will.

China, Japan, France, the UK and Canada are proponents for the inclusion of nuclear power within the CDM mechanism. France, which has the highest proportion of nuclear power within its energy mix, and the best record for nuclear safety of any of the developed countries, stands to benefit if nuclear is included as an option. Canada, which also has high marks for safety, would also benefit. Most importantly, though, the chance to incorporate China in the process of reducing greenhouse gases is of paramount importance. Taking Chinese coal-fired generators offline and replacing them with "green" nuclear fuel would benefit the world tremendously. On the opposing side of the argument are Greece, Italy, Sweden, Germany, Austria, Ireland and Denmark, plus the considerable power of the environmental lobby.

One of the big problems with nuclear energy is the cost of constructing a reactor and the time delay between planning and completion of the project. As an argument against nuclear power, Greenpeace quotes a World Bank study of electricity options in Thailand, claiming that nuclear power ". . . was not competitive to gas, lignite, coal or fuel-oil fired generation, even after the investment and operating costs of

[12] 'Q3 1999 – Europe's Nuclear Options', Wood MacKenzie Research Report.

pollution mitigating technology such as flue-gas desulphurization units on lignite and coal fired power plants were considered." This is one of the most disingenuous claims the organization has ever made, as they are, in effect, promoting the use of coal in power generation; even if the issue of global warming is discounted entirely, burning coal is still harmful for a plenitude of reasons. At any rate, environmental concerns are not big issues in Thailand, and it is self-evident that a country with an economy such as Thailand has no choice but to take the cheapest option when it comes to meeting their power needs. At current prices, a good sized nuclear reactor costs $1–2 billion to build, which, for a developing country like Thailand, is a lot of money. But if the economics of nuclear power were to change substantially, and a new generation of reactors were brought online that were inherently safe, it would definitely be an option under the CDM mechanism for foreign countries to build reactors on behalf of Thailand.

The demand for electricity in both the developing and developed worlds is skyrocketing. For most things in life electricity is the fuel of choice because it is clean (once it is produced), easily delivered, safe and versatile.

It is the goal of the world to provide modern energy services to virtually every person in the world. During the last decade, an additional 400 million people in the world have had their homes connected to an electricity supply. Since 1970, the total rural population in the world that is "electrified" has risen from 23% to 44%.[13] To bring the rest of the world up to modern standards will require connecting 100 million people a year for the next 20 years.[14] By electrifying the world, we can isolate pollution and work to control it. The uncontrolled burning of biomass to heat homes and for cooking not only degrades lifestyles, but

[13] M. Davis, 'Institutional frameworks for electricity supply to rural communities – a literature review', *EDRC*, University of Cape Town, 1995.
[14] *Energy for Tomorrow's World – Acting Now*, World Energy Council, 2000, p. 57.

also creates greenhouse gases. The world needs to find the technology to provide electricity to everyone, while still working to save the environment. Nuclear is one of the best options we have right now, and the new technologies, which are safer and cheaper, will have to be used to meet our demands.

Coal is in abundant supply in many of the countries that most need to produce cheap electricity. China, India, Indonesia and South Africa all have vast resources of coal, coupled with rapidly escalating power needs. The burning of coal throughout Asia is beginning to impact on agricultural production, as levels of acid rain have risen to intolerable levels. Unlike in western cultures, rural populations in Asia lack a political voice. The destruction of natural habitats and the degradation of the agricultural sector is seldom studied or brought to the attention of the government. When it is, it is not considered as crucial a priority as addressing the needs of the wealthier urban populations. The rural poor in the developing world are politically powerless. India and China are ideal sights for future large-scale hydro projects, but the potential to produce clean and cheap electricity from this source is mitigated by the environmental and social damage these projects produce. If these projects are supported by western nations seeking to earn carbon credits instead of utilizing cheap and safe nuclear alternatives, we effectively become accomplices in an evil trade.

If we are prepared to accept the use of radioactive substances for diagnosing and curing disease, making our food edible, and ensuring safety in our transport, why are we so scared of harnessing its power?

8

FUEL CELLS

As a wide-eyed environmentalist told us before we began this book, if we wanted to know all about global warming all we had to do was "follow the money". He, of course, thought we would follow a money trail to the end of the rainbow, where the whirring of windmills filled the air. What he failed to realize is that there are two types of money being spent on this problem: soft money and hard money. There is a huge difference between subsidizing the cost of a few watts of wind-powered electricity and a $500 million investment by Daimler Benz. There is also a big difference between governments throwing a few million dollars into research grants to explore the potential of biomass power, and the US Department of Defense underwriting a $100 million strategic investment. If you are interested in "following the money" in the global warming game, the trail is fairly well marked. It will lead you right to the western coast of Canada, and to the offices of Ballard Power Systems in Vancouver. Ballard is the firm that is sitting on the technology that could solve a major portion of this problem immediately. As opposed to the dot-com miracles of the past few years, Ballard is an industrial company that actually makes something that is fairly unique, and most of the world will have an intimate knowledge of this product in a few years. The one thing we should tell you right now, though, is that fuel cell development is being driven not by a desire to be green but by hard business logic. The fact that it happens to be green as well is what makes it so special.

Fuel cells have been in the public consciousness ever since the Apollo Program. We know they generate electricity using hydrogen and oxygen, and produce water as a waste product, which seems infinitely better when compared to the host of pollutants and greenhouse gases that spurt out of the tailpipe of a car. Beyond this, the public knowledge about fuel cells is limited, and this is probably for a good reason. Fuel cells may end up saving the world and they may represent the hottest investment opportunity since Microsoft was founded, but the truth is they are just very, very good batteries. And when was the last time you were fascinated by a battery? The sex appeal will come when that battery is applied to power the hottest cars on the road.

Fuel cells have no moving parts, make no noise, and require virtually no maintenance. The core component of a fuel cell is a multilayered plate, consisting of two electrodes separated by a solid polymer membrane electrolyte, through which hydrogen and oxygen pass. By passing through the plate, the hydrogen fuel breaks down into electrons and protons, and the free electrons are conducted as an electrical current. The amount of power each plate produces depends on its size and surface area. Plates are essentially stacked on top of each another in order to increase power. The amount of electricity a fuel cell generates is determined by the size and number of plates that are stacked together. A small hand-held fuel cell may produce an output of 100 watts, while a larger fuel cell comparable in size to a large packing crate generates around 250 kW of electricity.

In an ideal world, like the one that NASA aims for, fuel cells would run on hydrogen. We say "ideal" because pure hydrogen gives a fuel efficiency of almost 90%,[1] and the only waste product is water. Unfortunately, in the real world, pure hydrogen is difficult to isolate, hard to store, and one of the most volatile substances on earth. It exists in abundance on earth, but is always chemically bonded with other elements, mainly carbon as fossil fuels and oxygen as water. So, until we find ways of commercially isolating and storing pure hydrogen in a safe manner, we will have to settle for second best. In the real world, then, fuel cells are being designed to run on various hydrogen-rich substances, including natural gas (methane), gasoline and alcohols (methanol and ethanol). These substances are not as good as pure hydrogen, but they are still streets ahead of the internal combustion engine in terms of efficiency and emissions.

Virtually every car maker in the world is gearing up to convert a significant portion of their vehicles from internal combustion engines to fuel cells. Ford has taken a 15% stake in Ballard and allied themselves with Daimler Benz in the development of fuel cell powered cars. General Motors expects to have a fuel cell car "production ready" by 2004. BMW is developing a different type of fuel cell running on solid oxide technology. Other car companies that have made a commitment, backed by hard cash, include Renault, Peugot, Volkswagen, Toyota, Mazda, Honda, Nissan, Mitsubishi, Daewoo and Hyundai. The US Department of Defense is funding the development of fuel cells to power submarines and surface ships, and is purchasing high-powered units to provide portable electricity supplies in battlefield conditions. US and Canadian utilities and municipalities are also beginning to purchase large fuel cell power units to provide coverage during electrical demand surges. The market capitalization of Ballard is about $8 billion, and other competitive companies are valued in the $1–2 billion ranges. The valuation of these companies is not really related to their green potential. Even if there

---

[1]   Note that the standard internal combustion engine is only 30% efficient. By this we mean that only 30% of the potential energy is converted into motion; the rest is wasted as heat and noise.

were no threat of global warming, these businesses would be viewed as the wave of the future.

If we think of the fuel cell business as being analogous to the computer industry in its infancy in the 1960s, we can get a sense of the real potential of the business. In fact, making a fuel cell is so remarkably like making a computer that we can see instantly how the business may be structured in the future. As each fuel cell is limited electrochemically to produce something in the range of 1.2 volts, producing more voltage means simply stacking one on top of the other in much the same way that the density of transistors on a computer chip affects its power. A big stack of fuel cells produces a lot of power. The wattage produced depends upon the surface area of the cell, so a big, wide stack produces more power than a small, thin stack. Once the technology for the fuel cell is developed, and they can be made by machine, it is simply a matter of stacking the cells in the right manner to produce the desired power.

Production of fuel cells is limited now to a few firms, and they are still essentially hand-made. The patents for the technology start running out by the end of this decade, so the developers have a big choice on their hands. They can either license production, just like IBM licensed the production of its PCs, or they can hold on to the technology until the patents run out. If they license production, fuel cells will be made in much the same way, and in the same sort of factories, as computer memory chips are made. Once this occurs, economies of scale will be instantly achieved.

Given the apparent simplicity of the fuel cell compared with the complexities of the modern internal combustion engine, it is remarkable that we have yet to incorporate this technology within the transportation sector to any great extent. Innovation is ongoing, but to understand the progress that has been made, all we have to know is that Ballard only made the decision to commercially produce power cells in 1989. Less than seven years later they were being used in buses and experimental cars, and will be introduced in the mainstream automotive business in this decade. Just like the computer industry, innovation will be swift and ongoing, and each new generation will produce more power at greater efficiencies. It is estimated that with additional technology, fuel cells can by 90% efficient by 2010, even running on fossil fuels.

One of the major reasons why Ford and Daimler Benz collectively own 35% of Ballard is that they know the dynamics of the automotive business are going to change. In the future the buyer will be more interested in the branding of the power source and the electric motor than they will be in the identity of the body and frame of the car. How quickly can the power kick in? How responsive will it be to the accelerator? How smooth will the gradient be? Ballard is not an unambitious company. It wants to be seen as the future Intel of the automotive industry and to have its logo displayed prominently on each car, in the same way that "Intel" and "Pentium" are ubiquitous on every desktop and laptop computer. So the front of the car will carry both the Ford and the Ballard logos.

As anyone who has seen the inside of a new high-spec car knows, screens and silicon chips are increasingly finding their way in. With the fuel cell, all this gadgetry will have a better, more reliable source of power. And given that all this technology is now talking to an electric motor rather than a petrol engine, it is likely that there will be further massive improvements. So, the first big push will see state-of-the-art, powerful cars that will sell for what is under the hood. At last you will be able to hear the music on the in-car entertainment system properly without the sound of the engine interfering.

The point we are making is that fuel cell-powered cars will be bought by people who could not care less about global warming; they will buy the car because it is better than anything else around. Yes, fuel cells will be used to power large tractor–trailers, buses and trains, but to make inroads into the mass car market, which is what is required if they are to help us solve the problem of global warming, then they will have to capture the top end of the market.

We stated earlier that fuel cells were currently being designed to run on natural gas, gasoline and alcohols. In the early stages of the market, the most important thing is that when someone buys a fuel cell-powered car, they also have easy access to the fuel that goes in the tank. This means leveraging off the existing gasoline station infrastructure, which is designed for storing and delivering liquid products, hence ruling out natural gas. The obvious use of this infrastructure is to create fuel cells that run on gasoline, but if we jump ahead, what would be the fuel of choice? The most appropriate would appear to be ethanol, for a whole host of reasons. Firstly it is a liquid, which means that it can easily be supplied through the existing fuel infrastructure. It is also less toxic than gasoline and methanol, so in the event of pillage it will lead to less damage. More importantly, ethanol can be produced from biomass. The two crops that are currently used are corn and sugar cane, which are fermented in much the same way as other alcohols are made. There is a precedent for running cars on ethanol in the USA and Brazil. In the USA, firms produced what was referred to as "gasohol", a blend of gasoline (90%) and ethanol (10%), as a way of reducing dependence on imported oil during the time of high oil prices. In theory, the proportions could have moved even further in ethanol's favor, but that would have meant retuning car engines. Brazil had the most successful program, where cars were converted to run entirely on ethanol produced by the fermentation of sugar cane. In Brazil's case, the fall in oil prices and discovery of their own oil changed the economics.

When ethanol was first spotted as an octane enhancer, the refineries tried creating it themselves by reacting ethylene with water, but this proved inefficient and they chose to use ethanol produced by fermentation. So, if the fuel of choice is ethanol, then the knock-on effects will be enormous. Currently, about one-third of each barrel of oil is converted into gasoline, and yet more is consumed as diesel. If this demand was to fall away, this effectively reduces demand for crude oil by 35–40%, which would have dramatic effects for both oil producers and refiners. It is worth a minor digression here to think about the refinery process.

Crude oil is not a single compound, like water or ethanol, but a mixture of thousands of different compounds. In the same way as water and oil boil at different temperatures, so the various compounds in crude oil boil and evaporate at different temperatures. The starting point in an oil refinery is to put the crude oil into a distillation column, which heats the mixture. The first compounds to evaporate are collected together as gases. The next batch goes off to make gasoline. And we carry on like this, collecting jet fuel, heating oil, etc. until we are left with the residue at the bottom of the barrel. It will probably not surprise you to learn that the compounds that evaporate first are the small, light ones, and what we are left with in the residue are the really heavy compounds. And this is where it gets clever. Since the residue is worth very little, over the years scientists have developed various means of using pressure, catalysts and temperature to break up the compounds in the residue. The residue is literally broken into smaller pieces, and because they are smaller these can then effectively be mixed in with the other light compounds we got from the distillation column. The objective of all this is to produce as much of the valuable parts as we can, and be left with as little residue as possible. And given the enormous demand for gasoline, this has been the main focus of attention.

But it is not just demand that makes gasoline different. The refiners also have to think about car performance and the emissions produced. For instance, gasoline has to burn in a way that gives power without causing engine knock. Composition also has to be varied with the seasons to make sure that enough of the fuel vaporizes in the engine to ignite, but not so much as to cause vapor lock. Of all the products a refinery produces, gasoline is the one that generates the revenues. The other products – jet fuel, feedstock for the petrochemical industry, gases, and heating oil of various grades – just do not have the same demand as gasoline. So, if this demand for gasoline and diesel suddenly disappears, the refineries will need to significantly rethink their strategies.

Even if we assume for a moment that the oil industry comes up with an alternative fuel at a price that is irresistible, we believe that there would be domestic pressure in many countries in favor of ethanol created from fermented crops, and that this would become the fuel of choice. In the USA, it is estimated that ethanol production currently provides around 55 000 jobs, particularly in rural areas of the country, but this is a fraction of what it could be. Combine this with greater energy independence and cleaner emissions from a renewable source of energy and we have an irresistible alternative to fossil fuels.

There is a massive oversupply of sugar on the international markets. For tropical countries with no petroleum resources, ethanol can be produced cheaply and with little technical expertise. Given the increased efficiencies that can be gained using the fuel cell as opposed to the internal combustion engine, the economies of using ethanol will finally fit. From an environmental perspective, ethanol is carbon neutral. Buckminster Fuller would have described ethanol as "stored solar energy". The raw material used to make the fuel is grown using solar energy in the form of photosynthesis, which converts CO_2 to oxygen, while producing sugar compounds and fibrous material. The crops soak up carbon from the atmosphere and emit the same amount of carbon back into the atmosphere in the process of producing power.

We have spoken a lot about the refiners, but what about the producers? There will still be a need for oil, but the demand and hence the price will fall. Note that even if the fuel cells are powered by gasoline, if the engines are three times as efficient this translates into a fall in demand for crude oil of about 20%. This is, of course, on top of other downward pressures we have discussed elsewhere in the book. The worst hit will clearly be the Organization of Petroleum Exporting Companies (OPEC), who derive all their incomes from sales of crude oil.

We have digressed slightly from the subject of fuel cells and into the fuels that may be used because it is the fuels, and the source of the fuels, that will determine their effect on global warming. This will also have a knock-on effect through major established industries.

The introduction of the fuel cell will also impact the entire car repair and servicing sector. Although everyone will still need new brakes, shock absorbers and tires, actual engine repair will drop to nothing. The only possible servicing required may be to remove carbon build-up within the cell. The improved fuel efficiency will decrease the need for frequent tank refills, and this will reduce the need for service stations.

The fuel cell allows any one country to meet and exceed its CO_2 reduction targets cheaply and intelligently, while improving the quality of life for its citizens. Meeting targets by providing intelligent individual choices means less pressure will be brought to bear on industry and the price of emissions will be reduced. Fuel cells may reduce pollutants and greenhouse gases, reduce noise in urban areas, and have all kinds of other benefits, but the choice to use this technology to replace the internal combustion engine will be made because of economics. The process could use a little kick start to make it happen faster, but it will happen anyway.

The US government could make a simple choice tomorrow that would not involve a commitment of new funds, but would hasten the introduction of this technology across the board by at least five years. America is now in negotiations with Russia to buy its hot air credits, either by a debt swap or by purchasing them with hard cash. The government has eight years to meet a compliance target and has made no effort to curb emissions to date. By simply entering into an agreement with the major auto makers in America to convert its fleet of cars to fuel cell technology under relatively harsh guidelines, the government could provide the basis for this industry to switch to mass production methods that would produce quality products for the civilian sector. It could jump-start the widescale introduction of fuel cells in the transportation sector that may reach a critical mass eight years down the line, allowing the USA to withdraw from the hot air trade with Russia and sink the money into more effective domestic programs.

The USA is not the only nation that has this option. The first country that pushes this technology, funds it and produces it on a mass scale will develop an international market for its products and develop a lot of intellectual capital on the way. Canada is already home to a lot of this intellectual capital, and the provision of an interest-free loan to build the first mass-production plant for fuel cells would assure that the jobs the industry creates will remain in the country. Germany and Japan also have a lot invested in this technology, and both have long histories of government and industry co-operation that could help create a structure that lets the public sector share some of the risk in the venture.

The speed by which the fuel cell car is introduced into the developing world will be predicated on only one factor: price. If the technology to manufacture the components for the fuel cell is licensed, then manufacturing will naturally move to those countries that have excelled in the manufacture of the computer memory chip. These countries will be Korea, Taiwan, Singapore and China. They have highly technical work forces, but wages are competitive compared with Europe and America. If this is allowed to happen, prices for the basic cell will function solely on a supply-and-demand basis and costs will be low.

9

TRADING

There is morality and then there is money, and the two do not necessarily go hand in hand. Sometimes it is not always clear whether an action motivated by money is moral or not, and nothing illustrates this better than one particular financial "transaction" that existed in the USA in the late 1980s and early 1990s. During this period, Aids was spreading rapidly in the gay community in America, and there was no short- or long-term treatment for the disease on the horizon. An HIV positive blood test amounted to a death sentence, a process lasting six months to a year, and in its final stages, a variation of pneumonia was typically the cause of death. Naturally, those who tested HIV positive were desperate for any experimental drugs that could delay the onset of Aids, but these drugs were not sanctioned by any insurance companies. As a result, the infected individuals often had to fund experimental treatment from their own savings. As their savings dwindled to nothing, so did the opportunities of finding some means of arresting the course of the disease. As would happen only in America, capitalism came to the rescue. A mini-industry was created that bought the life insurance policies of desperate HIV positive patients at discounted prices and sold them on to investors.[1] The sick individual was provided with instant cash and the investor took a medium-term risk, which potentially provided a phenomenal payoff. In lieu of an analyst's report, which would normally be the basis for an investment in stocks or bonds, the investor received a detailed diagnosis from the patient's doctor estimating the remaining lifespan of the policyholder. Those who were in the most advanced stages of the disease and closest to death had different risk profiles to those who had been diagnosed with the disease recently. In a perfect society this sort of transaction would be both morally despicable and impossible.

Perhaps the fact that most of the investors who took advantage of this trade ended up being badly burnt provides anecdotal evidence that there may be a God out there after all. A combination of drugs was developed shortly thereafter that arrested the progress of the disease, and many of the individuals who were once considered hopelessly terminal cases are leading relatively healthy lives today. For the purposes of this book, this example has been used to put into context what should be considered a morally questionable trade. There are plenty of examples of what are clearly morally wrong transactions, for example underwriting arms sales to dictatorships, but trading the right to pollute is not one of these. It is, in fact, a perfect example of a "good" trade because although traders and banks may make money out of it, the rest of the world benefits too, as we will illustrate. In the real world, we have to use the tools that are available, whether or not they are perfect, and at this point in time capitalism appears to be the best we have.

Most people have the same gut reaction to any sort of problem, whether it is a toothache, a leak in the roof or dirty air. They want the problem to go away as quickly and simply as possible. It seems logical just to mandate instantaneous change, rather than waste time while invest-

---

[1] These are known as "Viaticle Investments", and not unsurprisingly have been the domain of some of the most unscrupulous investment sales companies in the USA.

ment bankers spend a few decades trading the problem away. Although this does seem logical, the command economy of the old Soviet Union also seemed more logical to many people than the disorganized mess of capitalism. Mandating instantaneous change would, in fact, immediately reduce greenhouse gas emissions, but it would simultaneously obliterate the economies of the industrial world. In real terms, it would make the Great Depression seem like the good old days. Trading our way out of the problem may not be the most ideal solution, but it is cheaper than the other alternatives, and it is almost righteously moral. Maybe the problem is one of semantics: if we started saying "clean air credits" rather than "emission credits", the concept might be palatable from the onset.

One of the oldest and most loved concepts in economics is that if the marginal prices of products differ between regions, then trade between these regions makes everyone better off. In the context of this problem, there are no products, but there are solutions that create value. Even though the majority of the population of the world is outside the confines of the Kyoto Protocol, the CDM mechanism allows them to reap the benefits of change. Assuming that the will of the industrialized world does not falter, we are about to witness a dramatic transfer of wealth to the developing world. We have the freedom to choose our battlefields. Making a significant dent in the level of emissions from a Latin American or Asian country will cost a fraction of the money it would take to significantly change emission levels in Germany or America. For investors who are financing these projects, a lot of the problems that accompany emerging markets investment are removed. The problems of political, credit and currency risk are irrelevant as the return on investment will be internationally recognized emission credits, which will exist even if the country slips into anarchy or devalues its currency by a factor of 100. Although the power sector will be the primary initial target for investors, an upgrade in local capacity will provide a reliable backbone upon which developing economies can prosper. Most importantly, if the structure behind the emissions trading market is strong enough, it will not be taxpayers' money funding this change. Institutional and private investors will be attracted by the potential returns from the market. Public money can be saved for investment domestically within Annex I countries.

Although planting forests in the hope of "capturing" carbon seems more moral than building a nuclear power plant, the reality is that if we start certifying forests as legitimate repositories of carbon, we create a new passive investment instrument that does nobody any good. An investment in a carbon sink does the world economy about as much good as buying gold and hiding it under the bed. A forest does not employ people on the same scale as a power plant, and it does not benefit the world in the same way that clean and cheap electricity transforms the life for the residents of the cities of the developing world. The most moral CDM projects will not only do the most to clean up emissions; they will also do the most to improve the lives of the world's most desperate people.

The American purchase of "hot air" from Russia is also questionable, but in the grand scheme of things it is not much more devious than the UK claiming it has met its quota of cuts by converting its electrical production from coal to gas. That transition was on the cards anyway, regardless of the edicts in the Kyoto Protocol. The official US and UK positions may be a bit disingenuous, but they are far from being morally wrong.

In fact, both of these examples have less to do with morality and more to do with ineptitude. The manner in which emission targets were set took little into account except the level of emissions at a certain point in time. The cost of change was never analyzed, nor was any attention paid to economic performance or forecasts. Given the sheer scale of the enterprise, distortions were likely to occur, at least initially. The reality is that every market is inefficient at the outset, but these inefficiencies are ironed out over time and eventually a transparent, fair and effective market is created.

It is morally questionable for Americans to be so in awe of their economic success that they lapse into a love affair with themselves and ignore their global responsibilities. It is equally questionable for General Motors to introduce the Hummer and speak proudly of expected sales, when they know what the environmental impact that 100 000 of these oversized converted military jeeps on civilian roads will be. But what is most amazing is for certain Americans to think that, somehow, the environment in which they live is disconnected from the rest of the world. In an article that appeared in the *Wall Street Journal*,[2] it was seriously argued that global warming "would benefit most Americans", although in developing countries "farmers earn too little to survive a shift to new conditions." The journalist added that, on the whole, "Global change is inevitable. Warmer is better. Richer is healthier." To take a line of reasoning that accepts that warmer winters are good because they mean longer growing seasons in Iowa, and that the cost of a few hundred million lives lost in Bangladesh justifies this economic gain, is crossing the line from morally questionable to immoral.

Nothing in this world is perfect. A solution to the problem of global warming must be practical. And by simplifying the problem and attaching a monetary value to it, the solution becomes perfectly clear to all. Given this, we believe that it is morally correct to set up a trading market in pollution, value the right to pollute on the open market, and use the financial power of the world's capital markets to finance projects that eradicate the problem and improve the lot of the world. In addition, we also believe that there will be positive side effects for the non-Annex I countries.

Whether it is moral or not to trade in pollution credits should not be the real question. The questions we should ask are, is this the best solution to the problem? Is the creation of a massive new bureaucracy

[2]   Thomas Gale Moore, 'Happiness is a warm planet', *Wall Street Journal*, 7 October 1997.

that monitors and verifies each transaction really necessary? Is there a better way to clean up the atmosphere than to hold yearly negotiations between 180 nations that set new limits and create reams of paperwork full of new regulations, rules and procedures? Is this process really about cleaning up the atmosphere or more about institutionalizing a scientific theory? Most importantly, what is the political risk of burdening business and local governments with a host of new rules and regulations? The negotiators and environmental ministers that convene together every year under the auspices of the UN have never had to run a successful power utility or energy company. Although their intent is to solve a problem, they are not the ones who will have to develop the solutions. Creative minds look at laws not as absolutes but as impediments that can be avoided, ignored or circumscribed. Verification is a subject rarely spoken about, although the first issue any layperson would recognize is the difficulty of verifying the total level of emissions each country, company or individual emits into the atmosphere. Trading emission credits is not a bad idea, and serves a limited purpose, but there is a downside to it as well. It creates a new cost to business that will be passed on to the consumer, further complicates the lives of every citizen of the Annex I countries, and creates numerous opportunities for avoidance and cheating. For trading to work, the market should be as simple and transparent as possible. Trading should be restricted only to those companies that publicly release audited data that confirm their financial figures and environmental responsibilities.

If the citizens of all the Annex I countries were given a choice tomorrow as to whether they wanted to live a poorer life in order to save the world from global warming, or to ignore the problem and grow wealthier by the day, is there really any doubt as to which choice they would make? This is an immutable fact, and it is what the conservative press has launched upon to stymie the entire process. What makes the issue so dangerous is the very subtlety of the problem. There is very little an individual can do personally to lower the temperature of the atmosphere, stop the ice caps from melting, or prevent severe weather events. Why should a Canadian cut back on heating if the Americans are doing nothing? Tackling global warming requires a collective response, which requires a degree of selflessness from us all. When the issue starts hitting the wallets of each and every one of us, a political resistance will build up that will be exacerbated if it is perceived by the taxpayers that they are saddled with a burden that is disproportionate to the rest of the world. We may pride ourselves on being good world citizens, but consider how each and every one of us votes on the day-to-day issues that affect the environment.

We know drinking aluminum cans of soft drinks is not ecologically sound. We should be taking our own shopping bags to the supermarket to be refilled. And we should all have a moral commitment to take public transportation all the time. Let's face it, there is an awfully big club of people out there who profess to care about the world but make choices every day that contradict that belief. If we are perfectly honest, if it came down to any really serious lifestyle choice, global warming would simply be a fact we accept, not an issue we are trying to address. The conservative press has rightly recognized this contradiction and, by exaggerating the economic impact of change, is building up some political resistance to compliance for even the first round of modest cuts. The point they are making is not entirely unjustified, as it is hard to see how this issue is going to create wealth for the world. It is particularly hard to see how the average American is going to be anything except worse off, unless an entire new mindset is used to address the issue. And if the Americans are hit too hard in their wallets and decide to withdraw from the process, the rest of the world might just as well start booking summer holidays in Greenland.

While the Kyoto targets are not being promoted as a tax, they quite blatantly are. In a simplistic sense, to cut emissions will cost money, and that cost will be passed on to the consumer. Perhaps the easiest and best example to use is to consider what effect this will have on a power producer who burns natural gas. In order to promote conservation, the simplest thing governments can do is to push the price of power up. When this happens, demand will fall, and when overall demand for a product falls, its intrinsic value falls as well. As the vehicle the government will use to push conservation is tax, a fall in the value of gas will be offset by the additional tax, a tax that will not apply in the non-Annex I countries.

The end result will be that in Annex I countries there will be an increase in the cost of energy and a decrease in consumption, while non-Annex I will benefit from lower world prices and see an increase in demand. And so the effect of additional taxation will potentially lead to a fall in the gross domestic product (GDP) of Annex I countries and growth in the GDP of non-Annex I countries. This is a fairly simplistic view of the world, but it is one that most people can grasp immediately. It is this simplistic view that is being played out by the conservative press to scare the electorate.

Whenever governments tinker with economic formulas, there are side effects, and this case is no different. A company that is a high emitter of greenhouse gases, and a big user of energy, will feel a dynamic pull towards non-Annex I countries, which offer cheap fuel, cheaper labor and virtually no environmental constraints. The individuals themselves in non-Annex I countries will also benefit from cheaper fuel, and will likely increase consumption. In addition, there will be other inward investments into non-Annex I countries coming from CDM projects. Investments will be drawn to countries that have, at the minimum, a stable rule of law, such as Egypt or India. These are real business decisions, not aid projects, and companies will be looking for the highest return on their dollar within reasonable risk constraints. CDM projects will be drawn to countries that not only provide a stable investment platform but are also best at marketing themselves as ideal host countries. For international investors, those countries most likely to be on the verge of joining Annex I will be attractive sites for CDM projects.

It is reasonable to assume that the lives of people in non-Annex I countries will be better off with the introduction of the protocol targeted cuts, but that over the medium and long term, they will eventually join Annex I. There are examples of countries that could be considered on the verge of entry, such as Argentina, Chile, Malaysia, South Korea, Taiwan and Uruguay. These are countries that are beginning to deliver middle-class lifestyles to their citizens. Their birth rates are down, they are politically stable, and there exists the freedom to express environmental concerns. This is not to say that these countries are intent on joining in the process, but their economic interrelationship with the rest of the world is such that there is a good degree of leverage the industrialized world can bring to bear over their political processes. If a country has reached the point in their development where environmental concerns are not survival issues, than they should be mature enough to be among the Annex I countries.

Each Annex I country faces a choice and the correct choice will result in an upturn rather than a downturn in GDP. At the extreme, a country has two ways in which it can fulfill its obligations under the protocol: simply buy credits from another country, or bite the bullet and make massive domestic investment. If they buy from another country they are effectively throwing money away: it buys time, but not a solution. If, on the other hand, the money is spent on infrastructure to reduce emissions, this is an investment and it creates jobs.

If America throws money at Russia, it simply delays the problem. This may be politically astute, but it is economically dumb. It is no secret that America's love affair with the car is its biggest problem. Getting Americans out of their cars is perhaps the most formidable challenge the world faces. It is virtually a constitutional right for Americans to drive anywhere, including the next-door-neighbor's house, and the only way to entice them to change is to present a better alternative. The only way to do this is to build state-of-the-art mass transit systems that deliver people to places they want to go in greater comfort, at less cost and in a more convenient manner than driving. If we look at Detroit, it is a case in point of a dying city. Detroit is now the impoverished hole in the center of a wealthy donut of industry and suburbs. It is dying because it has no economic value. Cities with good mass transit systems do not die. The economic value of a subway system is almost immeasurable. If we hearken back to the mid-1980s, New York was overrun by crime, and the executives of many of the Fortune 500 companies were sick to death of the place. They wanted an office within a short drive of their Fairfield County homes and, in a move that in retrospect must seem at best ill advised, they packed everything up and planted their new company headquarters in Stamford, Connecticut. Unfortunately, they forgot they were not the only ones working in the office. For the rest of the employees, getting to work was impossible. Those companies are still there and paying rewards to headhunters for second-rate secretaries on flexible work schedules. Meanwhile, their old offices in midtown have been rented to a new breed of companies who can take advantage of a vast pool of skilled workers that are delivered everyday to their door on time at a cheap price. An investment that improves the quality of life for the majority of its citizens and creates a long-term economic value for large municipalities should not be looked upon as a cost. Getting people off the roads in America is a big challenge, but the process will create jobs, make life better and add value.

As America invests in itself, it will also be investing in the far corners of the earth to finance change. It will be competing with Europeans and the Japanese for these same investments. Although money will seemingly be flowing right out of the developed world and into the developing world, this will be mitigated immediately by the fact that it will flow right back again to purchase the goods the developing world is so good at making.

To the most idealistic of the world – those who would like to see every citizen have the same standard of living as every other – there is some poetic justice in the wealth transfer that will occur during this century as proposed under the trading system. The trading of emissions, the creation of credits through CDMs, and the securitization of these credits in the capital markets are subtle mechanisms for pushing through change on a global scale. In some way, the most successful of the world are being made to atone for their sins. This is a thought that should raise the blood pressure of every Keynsian capitalist in the world. If we assume the process actually gets under way, and works in the way the architects of the plan envisioned, it does not necessarily mean that the developed world will become impoverished at the expense of the developing world. Capitalism is a great survivor, capable of mutating itself at various stages to deal with different environments. In this case, there will be a flow of money from the developed to the developing world, which then allows the developing world to purchase the developed world's products. The result is that American, British, French and Japanese manufacturers who make the technology vital to the world will also come out as winners. Trading may push through a transfer of wealth, but it may also be a vehicle that sells products, employs people and creates further wealth.

Just as the architect always gets to do the interesting part of building a new house, the fellow who first sticks his shovel in the ground invariably gets stuck with the most boring job. There must be a deep satisfaction that a certain type of individual gets from digging a hole, just as the adrenaline must rush through the veins of an accountant when the books are finally balanced. Our preference would be to be the one who gets to design the house, or who caused the financial calamity that made the books so difficult to balance. The last thing we would like to think of ourselves as being is boring and, as environmentally conscientious as we are, we would never want to be accused of using hundreds of pages of paper to state the obvious. In this instance, though, we are absolutely stumped. In order that you pause here and assess your own character, we have decided to ask you which of these two subject headings looks more interesting:

1. Before greenhouse gas emissions can be traded, the foundations of the market have to be created.
2. Killer ants destroy Japan!

If you chose number one, you better put your knitting down and hang on to your seat, because this book is just about to get really interesting. For the more frivolous readers out there who chose number two, we have to say we are a bit disappointed in you. The rest of this chapter is the ultimate test of character. Although we will try to make this as painless and brief as possible, we have to warn you that if you do not buckle down here and read this thoroughly, you will regret it the rest of your life.

For want of a better cliché, the best place to start out is the beginning, and that is at the point that emission credits are created. Most of us are familiar with stocks and bonds, and can grasp the concept of a share certificate signifying ownership. Each share certificate is numbered and registered somewhere. Carbon credits[3] are the same: they entitle the holder to something, but the register is in fact the Ministry of Environment, Department of Energy or some other government department.

Just as the UK is the undisputed leader of the world in marmalade production, the country is also ahead of the field in creating a market in emissions trading. For our purposes, we will use the UK as an example. Under the proposed system, there will be a central record of the credits

---

[3]   Note that we are going to use a lot of different names interchangeably just to keep you on your toes: emissions, carbon, CO_2, pollution ...

that exist, and a record of which company owns each one of them. When a credit is bought or sold in the market, the trade has to be reported to this central authority so that the records can be updated. To all intents and purposes this register is a bank.

In its most simplistic state, the New World will work something like this. Each year, power stations will be given their allocated number of credits. Every time they emit a ton of CO_2, a credit is surrendered.[4] And in the same way as an individual runs his or her own bank account, the aim is to stay in credit. In fact, in this instance getting overdrawn has severe penalties, because the interest rate on an overdraft will be extortionate.

For anyone who has bothered to read the previous paragraphs, it is blatantly obvious we actually did not start at the beginning. Tests like this will be thrown in regularly, not only for our own amusement, but also to test the conscientiousness of the reader. If we start all over again, even before the beginning, we realize that emission credits cannot actually be used before they are created. As we know, the Kyoto Protocol sets limits for each country. In the case of the UK, we know how much CO_2 the country is allowed to produce in 2010. It is now up to the UK government to ensure that the country as a whole comes in at or below that level. The government now has to use a mixture of constraints (for industry) and persuasion (for the public) in order to achieve their objective.

There are three principal ways that the credits can be allocated between the various companies: they can be auctioned off,[5] allocated by

---

[4] We are assuming here that the face value of one of the credits will be one ton of CO_2.

[5] In this case, "auctioning" simply means that the government sells the right to pollute to the various companies. On the face of it, this approach seems fair, and in theory it is the most efficient. The problem, however, is that it is effectively a tax: the power company, for instance, suddenly finds that the cost of generating has jumped.

"grandfathering",[6] or the levels could be agreed to by discussion.[7] In the UK, the main approach that has been taken is grandfathering, so the cuts are spread more or less evenly over those companies that were polluting in 1990. This is how the credits are allocated, and from that point they can be traded.

As we discussed before, the reason why trading is morally acceptable is that it is a proven means of minimizing the cost of achieving things. In this case, implementing the cuts ordained by the protocol. Since the government wants to put as little burden as possible on the economy, it wants trading to work and the costs for industry to be low. It is therefore in the government's interest to make sure the market is efficient, and that all interested parties have full access to information. The best way to achieve this is for the government[8] itself to organize the market, which will probably be in the form of an Internet-based trading system,[9] overseen by a central authority that acts as banker. Since the aim is to minimize costs, the government will want to remove all barriers to trade and create as much price transparency as possible.[10] In an organized regulated

[6]   Put simply, "grandfathering" uses history as the benchmark. If you polluted a lot in the past then you are given a lot of credits. This is really how the Kyoto levels themselves are framed: basis 1990.

[7]   Because this is based on discussion, rather than a simple formula, it should produce a good result. The drawback is that the negotiations could take a long time. On the positive side, it means that people have had a chance to have their say, and so they should buy into the process much easier. It also allows the government to put pressure on industries that have more scope to cut back.

[8]   Or, more correctly, an independent authority appointed by, and reporting to, the government.

[9]   In reality, there may be some sort of dedicated trading system created. At this stage it is not important what platform is used, only that information flows freely.

[10]   In most new markets, the control lies in the hands of a few players who jealously guard the information they have. This gives them an edge over new entrants, and allows them to make unusually high profits. In this case, though,

market, there is usually a set of daily prices. These could be set at close of business, last trade, weighted average, or some other valid point. The important thing is that these figures are independent of the "players" and distributed publicly.

The market we have been describing is the "physical" market, where people trade the right to put CO_2 into the atmosphere. This is a market for industry, not for banks. There is another market, quite separate, for which there are no credits, no centralized market place and no central register of delineating ownership. This is called the "over-the-counter" (OTC) market, and this is where it gets really interesting.

The market we have addressed so far fulfills two quite distinct functions. Firstly, it is a physical market – a way in which buyers and sellers can balance their books and ensure that they have enough credits to cover the pollution they are causing. The second function is a way of setting the price. In a physical industry, such as the oil market, you will find that these two functions are often dealt with by two separate departments. There will be the purchasing department that attends to the purchase of physical crude. This is the department that actually takes care of the physical running of the business. Oil companies also have financial departments, whose job it is, among other things, to ensure that the risk arising from changes in prices, be they exchange rates, interest rates or carbon credits, is controlled. When the emissions market begins, it will also be split into the physical side and the hedging side, and the hedging risk will be done on the OTC market.[11]

OTC markets are more complex than physical markets, but they

the market is being created by a single entity – the government – which is not driven by profit. It will therefore want to create a level playing field in order to remove the ability to make extraordinary profits. One of the things it will aim for is to ensure that all information is in the public domain.

---

[11] Strictly speaking, we should say "OTC derivatives", because the market we are about to describe is *derived* from the physical market.

cannot exist independently of a vibrant underlying market. In simple terms, OTC markets allow companies to lock in a price for the future, and banks merely intermediate this transaction. If a particular company (let us call them Power Inc.) wants to secure a future buying price for credits in December, they speak to a variety of potential counterparties. This is the same as shopping around for the best deal on that new car, except that rather than paying and taking delivery today, they are simply locking in a price for later on. Now let us assume that Power Inc. finds someone who agrees to sell the credits at $15 next December. If in December prices are $17 a ton, then Power Inc. buys in the credits in the market at $17 (this is the physical part), and also receives $2 from the counterparty (the OTC deal). The net cost to Power Inc. is $15. If, on the other hand, the price is $12, it will have to pay the counterparty $3, to compensate them for the fact that it can buy the physical credits at $12. So, no matter what happens to prices, the OTC market allows Power Inc. to lock in a particular price. Obviously, all this requires either a great deal of trust or an independent adjudicator. Since there is money involved, an adjudicator is required, and that is the reference point or index.

Once an OTC market is established, companies or speculators can take a position on prices going up or down. Speculation is essential as it provides day-to-day liquidity.

To understand how useful an OTC market is requires an understanding of the advantages it brings to the corporates who have to account for every ton of CO_2 they emit into the atmosphere. If one particular company is in credit in their emissions account, and the price of emission certificates falls, they will lose money. This is a risk that they are obliged to run because the authorities have dictated that they should always have enough credits to cover their emissions. In order to remove this risk, they will use the OTC markets to compensate them for a fall in prices. Then, if market prices fall, the money made in the OTC market makes up for the loss on the credits. Similarly, when prices rise, they lose money on the OTC market but make money on the physical market. The net position then is such that no matter what happens to prices, they neither gain nor lose. The OTC market then gives them the ability to run a surplus on the physical credits, but without the price risk, and allows them to manage their inventory more easily. The speculators, who are all too often painted in the most evil tones, actually perform an invaluable service: the more people there are in a market, the more likely a company will find a counterparty, and the better the price will be. The example we have cited is a little simplistic. There are a whole host of other reasons why a company may wish to use OTC markets, most of which have to do with the asymmetrical treatment of credit and deficit positions.

One of the points mentioned was the fact that the overdraft rate in this market will be extortionate. In the case of the system under proposal by the UK government, there is also a cost for running a positive balance: each company will have to surrender 1% of its banked deposits at the end of each year. The reason for this mechanism is that it enables the government to build a public fund of credits that can then be used by new entrants in the market, although it is also an asymmetrical treatment of the balance. At this early stage in the process, full tax and regulatory information is incomplete, although the UK government is doing its utmost to create a free market unfettered by onerous taxation. The negative affects of taxation and regulatory control in the US NOx and SOx markets have been noted across the Atlantic.

If all goes according to plan, then the next logical step is the introduction of "insurance"[12] on the price. In simple terms, the idea is that a company that needs to buy credits next year can buy insurance against the

---

[12] In the markets, these contracts are called "options" but they are exactly the same.

market going above a certain level.[13] If a price above $15/ton is painful for the company, it will be able to buy insurance that will reimburse it if prices rise above $15. If prices in the next year are $19/ton, the insurance contract will compensate it by paying $4; obviously if prices are lower than $15, then there is no payment.

There is one massive assumption made in all this, and that is that people will actually be interested in trading. The reality is that if there is price volatility, and it emanates from logical sources, then people will want to hedge their risks, they will want to out-smart the market, and they will want to speculate. The big question is, will there be volatility?

Until now, we have been drawing parallels between credits and banking as a way of illustrating various points. This is not something created out of our imaginations: the whole concept of banks and the banking of credits is enshrined in the Kyoto Protocol. This agreement has, in effect, created a new currency that can be deposited in a bank balance, and as a company pollutes, the account is debited. Companies that burn fossil fuels will be literally "burning money". If one particular company has a healthy bank balance with the UN, the question is how to translate this into real money.

If credits are an asset, they therefore need to be on the balance sheet of the company. When they are burnt, they will show up as a cost in the profit and loss account. OTC markets provide financial products that are considered neither an asset nor a liability because their value can be assessed only theoretically, depending upon which way the prices go. OTC contracts are termed as "off-balance-sheet" products, and physical products are referred to as "balance-sheet" items. If company accounts can be interesting, which they are not, the most intriguing item to look

[13] There are two types of insurance: against the market rising (called "call options") and against the market falling (called "put options"). These are standard market instruments for managing risk, and are in use in all financial markets.

for is the "sources and uses of funds" statement. In the standard annual report, the sources and uses account shows where the company got its cash from (sources) and what they did with it (uses). Sources and uses is all about cash. Most of us concentrate on the profit and loss statement but the fact of the matter is that the profit and loss account tries to cover all aspects of the health of the company, and so it is sometimes a little hard to see the wood for the trees. For an analyst that wants to delve below and really understand a business, it is important to know what is happening to the real cash, and this requires a good look at the sources and uses statement.

Given the nature of the carbon credits and the importance being attached to them, they are likely to be a focal point for environmental lobby groups, green funds and shareholders. Even if there is no legislation in place, moral and peer group pressure will ensure that a company makes public statements and eventually prepares accounts like a "sources and uses of carbon credits". This statement would tie in with other aspects of the "Triple Bottom Line"[14] idea that is currently being promoted. And from it we could derive various ratios, such as CO_2 emissions per megawatt hour, identify trend improvements, and perform peer group analysis. For a company that wants to stand up and claim to be green this is a logical strategy. But, more importantly, as investment funds and private investors focus on "green" companies, this will be a way of distinguishing those who care for the planet and those who just care about money. This will be the stuff the *Green Investor Weekly* feeds on in the future. If the investors are interested, it is a certainty that equity analysts will latch on to it, and companies will soon be rated on a scale of 1 to 10 as a guide to whether they are environmentally friendly or not.

Since there are funds that will invest only in green companies, the greener a company is, the more investment funds there will be chasing

[14] The Triple Bottom Line refers to economic, environmental and social performance.

their share price, which will drive market value. Similarly, the greenest companies will have more investors willing to lend money, which will equate to a lower interest rate. It is possible then that a company's greenness rating will be shown alongside the company's credit rating and, together with the value of the credits they hold, will become elements to be taken into account in take-over situations.

We have previously touched briefly upon the trading market that is being envisaged for the UK, and it should be clear from that discussion that the government is attempting to do two things. Firstly, of course, they want to create a domestic market that helps the country as a whole to meet its commitments under the protocol. But there is a second intention, and that is to help ensure that if trading between countries takes place, a UK credit is worth the same as a credit from another country. In other words, the UK and other countries must develop the trading framework so that it is *globally* applicable, which will then allow a UK company to buy or sell credits to Australian, American or Japanese companies.

To get this far means creating a globally fungible[15] market in emission credits; at the heart of this market will be the UN, who will validate the parameters of the market. It will undoubtedly happen, but each country will require domestic targets to be hit before they will be comfortable having their corporates buy or sell in the international arena.

Once we are in this position, the world opens up further, the credits become an asset class in their own right, and debtor nations will look upon them with increased interest. Russia, for example, does not have a world-class track record for honoring debt, although it is a big holder of unused emission credits, and in the short term, it will undoubtedly be on

---

[15] Fungible is a financial term that is used to distinguish two different items that are essentially the same and are treated in the financial markets as having the same value. A simple example would be the Scottish pound and the English pound.

the market selling these credits. The way this would work is very simple: Russia would borrow US dollars, and repay in the form of carbon credits. This only really works if the credits are a substitute currency, as we have discussed above. The clever part is that if you are one of the companies who are receiving the credits, once Russia has signed up, the rest of the process is down to the UN to simply reassign credits each year from Russia to the company. Russia cannot default. Of course, they may start polluting more than they should under the agreement, but this is then an international issue of a country not sticking to its commitment.

If you have an interest in the financial markets, and consider yourself something of a financial guru, here's an interesting puzzle. What would you estimate the cost of pollution to be in the year 2020? Before you make up your mind, pause for a moment and think of all the variables that enter into the equation. Even without the benefit of a scientific risk assessment, and the computing power of NASA, it is still startlingly simple to figure out the cost of pollution in 2020: it will have no value whatsoever. That may seem like interesting news, but what is much more interesting is figuring out how the world gets to that point. There are two possible courses the world could choose to follow in the intervening 20 years, both ending up at the same destination. The choice that is made will determine the sort of world we will live in during the next century.

By the year 2020, either the world will have decided to ignore the problem and accept the consequences, or we will have gone through a short period of pain during which time the industry will have developed a number of innovative solutions and the problem will be resolved. Either way, by 2020 cost of pollution will be free again.[16] Of course, if we choose to accept the problem, the quality of life will be pretty poor, but if we take the other alternative, it might not be a bad place at all.

[16] Note that the objective of the Kyoto Protocol is not to make us become monks when it comes to emissions, but simply to cut back to a level that nature can handle. The key phrase here is "sustainable energy", not "no carbon".

As the option to accept the problem is pretty horrific to consider, and we believe it is unlikely to occur, we will assume that the world will continue on with its effort. But for this to work we need companies not just to continue with their investments, but to step up the pace. This means creating the right environment for companies to invest, and removing the constraints that are continually being put in their way. And as far as the protocol is concerned, it would be sensible if the ground rules were laid out as soon as possible, and that management of the targets is done in an intelligent way. To understand this better, consider for a moment a mature market.

Long-term forecasting of yields on US government securities, or trying to second guess the stock market, is pretty difficult, but at least we know there is a group of individuals who have ultimate control over at least one segment of the market. The Board of Governors of the Federal Reserve Bank determines short-term interest rates, and thus has tremendous power over both the fixed income and equity markets. A spike in interest rates creates a tidal wave that washes through the entire economy. Fortunately, analysts have a host of information to assess the risk of this occurring, at least in the short and medium term, but how many people do you know who are brave enough to put themselves on the chopping block and tell us definitely what the cost of borrowing will be in 2020?

In terms of the emissions market, the "Board of Governors" is a loose coalition of politicians, special interest groups, bureaucrats, industrialists and, most importantly, environmental scientists. It is the latter that will hold sway, solely because they will be considered the most impartial arbitrators of the market. The "interest rate" will be a series of successive targets, each of which will be more difficult to meet. The difference is that the Fed has had years to perfect its fine tuning of interest rates. They avoid shocks; they slowly, gradually turn the screw, and they get where they want at an even pace without causing significant market volatility.

And the reason for this is not that they are terribly nice; it is simply that if they want people to invest in the future, they know that those people will either want stability or a huge premium. If most central banks are dominated by economists, and they regularly misjudge the market when setting interest rates, how on earth should we expect this collection of industrials, scientists and charities to do it properly? Part of this management process is ensuring that they cut effectively but do not upset the public. Again, this is similar to trying to slow down an overheated economy: if it is done too quickly, it plunges a country into a recession, and if it is done too slowly, it has no effect whatsoever.

In terms of cost, the first round of cuts will have little impact on the world, and a negligible effect on the economy. It is the second round of cuts that will hurt, and when these are announced, the yield curve for long-dated and short-dated emission credits will spike. Although these cuts will be announced in 2005,[17] there will be various leaks before that point that will affect price and economic planning. The challenge the world faces is to get through this first period in a way that makes the cost of change work for the good of all the Annex I countries' economies. This will be extremely difficult, because a wall of political opposition will build up that might very well get strong enough to halt the process entirely. And if the general public starts to notice the cost of the change in any significant way, the fight will be lost. In the USA, the political right is already comparing the cost of preventing climate change against the cost of accepting it and, as you will have no doubt guessed, they are pushing for acceptance of the latter alternative. This is not far from becoming a mainstream belief, and preventing this will be a big political challenge.

If we are to keep the cost of change down, then we need to avoid expensive, impractical solutions. This means that heavily subsidized industries, such as windmills, need to be avoided. Maybe this is a good time to differentiate between the two types of subsidies. There are

[17] 2005 is the latest they can announce cuts for the next commitment period.

subsidies handed out to develop an industry that is then self-sustaining, and there are subsidies that need to be handed out year after year because the project is fundamentally unsound. The objective should be to ensure that money is focused where solutions can be found, rather than misdirected to pacify pressure groups. Given the right motivation to develop a full set of new technologies, billions of dollars will be poured into the solution.

Another area of potential mismanagement comes from the regulatory framework. As a general rule, financial assets are less volatile than commodities because they are easier to store and manage. In other words, there is less in the way of physical, legal or financial constraints. This market is no different: the fewer constraints there are, the more orderly the market will be, and the easier it will be for companies to plan and invest.

Assuming that we can get all this regulatory market management stuff right, there are still obviously going to be shocks, as there are in any other market. One very important one, the one that we want, is downward pressure on prices resulting from technology shocks.

In case you feel the ground shifting beneath your feet, you will be pleased to know that technology shocks are not something we dreamed up after watching a science fiction movie. There is technology on the drawing boards right now that could resolve the problem. Global warming is a disease that is much easier to cure than Aids or cancer. Unlike a virus, the source of the disease will not continuously mutate. The variables are fixed, the source of the problem is public knowledge, and the solutions are simple. All the world has to do is significantly reduce the consumption of fossil fuels, or find a way to use these fuels that is not harmful. With the correct financial motivation, technology shocks will occur with regularity. There are a host of solutions to the problem, and when these are applied the threat of climate change will greatly diminish or disappear.

Waxing lyrical about the future is easy to do, but the bad news is that we live in today's world and we have to set up the foundation for implementing change and get the formula right. Very few people are involved in this process, and the rest of the citizens of the Annex I countries have to live with their decisions. Many analysts assume that CDM projects will not be a big factor, or they will be legislated out of the process. To do this would create an environment that would make it more politically difficult to sell the cost of change to the taxpayers. A large CDM project, such as a hydroelectric project in Africa, will produce the same savings in carbon emissions as a major domestic project, at a fraction of the cost. The CDM mechanism is a way to lower the cost of pollution, while still doing the world some good. This will work only if the UN does an effective job of certifying the projects. If we assume, as many have, that the number of CDM projects undertaken is relatively small, then they will have little impact on the supply of emission credits, and so figuring out the cost of abatement, and thus the cost of emission credits, is a fairly simple matter.

Prices per ton of CO_2 emitted into the air have been estimated to be anything from $6 to $30. Assuming that the actual price is around $15 a ton, it is interesting to see what will happen when variables change. Assuming a worst-case scenario in which the scientific community is convinced that radical reductions in emissions are required, the next round of cuts might be as high as 50%.[18] Virtually all industries will begin to stockpile emission credits, because common sense will tell them the price will go through the roof, and they will be right: their actions will drive up the price. To use some market jargon, the price will discount future expectations. The opposite will occur if the next target is negligible. The actual price we will see in the market before the next announcement will be the actual market view, unless of course one of the hundreds of bureaucrats happens to spill the beans to one of the thousands of interested parties.

[18] This is highly unlikely.

The degree of responsibility the government decides to throw at the industrial sector is another consideration that will severely impact cost. It is an easy decision for a politician to place the entire cost of reducing greenhouse gas emissions on the doorstep of industry. In so doing, they alleviate the need to shape the behavior of the electorate, who in fact contribute more to the problem than industry. In a democracy, the head of a major utility may be a powerful figure, but he or she still has only one vote. It will be pretty convenient for any country that has a reduction target of 5% across the board to put the entire problem into the laps of the people who only put one-quarter of the emissions in the air. In effect, they can force one sector of the country to reduce by 20% while the rest contributes nothing. For those industries that are mobile, the only option is to simply move production across borders. But for utilities, the only option is to bite the bullet and pass on the cost to the consumer. The politicians thus get to introduce a hidden tax for which they receive no blame. This scenario is not as unlikely as it sounds, and the result will be to further increase the cost of emission credits.

Under these scenarios, the cost of polluting is bound to rise over time, but it will be alleviated by technological shock as well as long-term investment, which will gradually resolve the problem. If nuclear energy is an option, the conversion of a significant portion of production will not be done overnight. Municipal and federal investment in infrastructure projects will also generate reductions over time. If the horizon begins to look more promising, there will be downward pressure on prices. Legislative mandates can have more immediate effects. Curtailing the use of cars by placing higher taxes on gasoline will have instantaneous effects on consumption and emissions. The more the government can do to get all sectors of society to reduce emissions, the less pressure it will have to place on industry. If the government generates regular forecasts, this information will enhance the abilities of companies to plan long-term projects.

In case you have not noticed, we have yet to give a real forecast on the price of carbon in the years 2001–2020. We did think long and hard about it, and came to the conclusion that our opinion on the price would be about as worthless as the paper it was printed on. We came to this conclusion for a couple reasons: the impossibility of applying theoretical models, and practical experience.

Economic theory states that the price of a product is based on its marginal cost, or simply the cost of producing one more of the item. In a unique twist on this economic theory, the value of emission credits is based on the cost of *not* producing one more of the product. In other words, the credits will be valued by the marginal cost of abatement. But does anyone have the slightest clue as to how much it will cost to "abate" a ton of CO_2 in Africa or rural parts of China? This may sound like a frivolous excuse for avoiding a hard question, but the reality is that these are areas where CDM projects could be implemented, and that could affect the price. It is important to differentiate between what *could* affect the price and what *will* affect the price. The market price will not reflect the actual cost of abatement, but will reflect what people think the cost of abatement will be, and that can be quite different. Sometimes in financial markets, an upward price move is justified quite simply as "there are more buyers than sellers". Now whilst this statement is of no value, it is true: at a certain price, more people feel motivated to buy, and so the price goes up. The price reflects views, which can depart a long way from reality.

The only viable comparison by which an analyst can judge the future price of carbon is the NOx and SOx market in the USA. This market was put in place in 1990 in order to restrict emissions of sulfur dioxide (SOx) and nitrous oxides (NOx) as a way of reducing acid rain. The following is a brief extract from a discussion paper published in 1997, where the authors compare expectations and experience of the price of SOx:[19]

[19] Douglas R. Bohi and Dallas Burtraw, *SO₂ Allowance Trading: How experience and expectations measure up*, Resources for the Future, February 1997.

Prior to the enactment of the Clean Air Act Amendments in 1990, the estimated price of allowances ran as high as $1500, a number that was enshrined in the Act as the fixed price of direct sales by the EPA [Environmental Protection Agency]. During 1990, the EPA cited a price estimate of $750 as the best guess of what allowances (and emission reductions at the margin) would cost.

Instead, actual prices for inter-utility trades have been considerately lower, starting out in the range of $250–300 in 1992, they fell steadily to $110–140 in 1995, and to around $70 in 1996 before rebounding to the low $90s at the time of this writing.

These analysts got it completely wrong in an environment where there was a single market, a single regulator and a single flexibility mechanism, and where companies know each other and have a fair idea as to how events are going to unfold. With this in mind, it seems a little unlikely that we can have the slightest idea as to what the price of carbon credits will be when they start to trade. One thing is for sure: there will be a significant amount of volatility in the early days, with little in the way of actual trades being done. During this time the market will slowly absorb the ideas and biases of the individual participants, and a clearing price will emerge. If this consensus price deviates too far from the actual cost of abatement, then the difference will be brought back into line by the traders and investment bankers exploiting the difference.

10

METHANE AND OTHER
GREENHOUSE GASES

So far, we have concentrated on CO_2 as the main greenhouse gas for a couple of reasons. The first reason is that it is something we can do something about, and the second is that production of CO_2 is going to grow rapidly as the world gets richer and people consume more energy. We would be remiss if we just stopped there, though, because there are a few other things going on that we should study. CO_2 is just one of the Big Six gases cited by the Kyoto Protocol. While CO_2 accounts for 60% of the problem, the other gases are actually much more toxic; thankfully, the level of emissions of these gases is minute in comparison with CO_2.

Of the Big Six, three are naturally occurring greenhouse gases. These include CO_2, methane (CH_4) and nitrous oxide (NOx). The other three are man-made gases: hydrofluorocarbons (HFCs), perfluorocarbons (PFCs) and sulfur hexafluoride (SF_6).

Most of the emissions of CO_2 can be laid down clearly to a simple cause and effect relationship: we burn and we create gas. This is not the entire cause of CO_2 emissions, though. About one-quarter of the CO_2 enters the atmosphere through land use change, and a further 3% can be accounted for by cement production.

Reducing certain emissions of CO_2 is difficult, solely because in some cases there is no substitute for that particular industrial process; the worst of these processes by far is the way in which cement is made. We can understand that you probably have not thought much about cement in your life, but everyone should at least know what makes cement different from concrete. Concrete is the finished product. It is made by mixing together cement, sand and gravel. Cement is the binding element in the mixture and makes up 12% by weight of the concrete. When concrete hardens, it is actually going through a chemical reaction called "hydration". Studying this process is electrifying and, as it is something we would not want you to miss, we will discuss it in a moment. In the meantime, though, we should look at the process behind making cement and understand why this industry contributes such a disproportionate amount of greenhouse gases to the atmosphere.

The basic ingredients for making cement are calcium and silicon, which come from limestone (calcium carbonate) and clay or sand (silicon). These substances are heated up and mixed together in a rotary kiln. These kilns are in fact the largest moving industrial equipment on earth. The temperature rises to about 1500°C. At around 900°C, the limestone changes into lime by shedding vast quantities of CO_2. This process is called calcining. The lime and sand continue to heat up, and when they are in a molten state they combine chemically to produce cement. Thus CO_2 is produced in two ways: from the calcining process and from the burning of fossil fuels to generate the intense heat required to melt the two substances together. Estimates vary, but the consensus is that the process used to produce a ton of cement also produces one and a quarter tons of CO_2, 40% of which comes from the calcining process.

Let us now return to the hardening process. There are ways to reuse the CO_2 emitted in the process of producing cement, but these methods may not be practical in the real world. If cement is cured in a CO_2-rich atmosphere, it not only absorbs great quantities of this gas, but it reaches its full potential strength much faster than through conventional curing. It is estimated that up to 80% of the CO_2 emitted during the calcining process could be reabsorbed during the curing process. As concrete is seldom cured in the laboratory, this may not be a practical solution. Cement is poured as a liquid on construction sites and left to cure for periods of up to 30 days. There is some production of prefabricated steel and concrete building materials, and curing the cement in a CO_2-rich environment might work in this process.

Of the heat used in the kiln, 95% comes from burning fossil fuels. The intense heat produced in the kiln is the perfect environment for destroying toxic wastes, including paint residues, printing inks, used car oils, tires, solvents and medical waste. There is virtually no other alternative to using fossil fuels to make cement, short of placing a nuclear reactor next to every plant.

Cement is something we need in the modern world to construct buildings, roads and sidewalks. We cannot penalize this industry, as many would like to do, unless another alternative method of making a similar building material is found, or a different method of producing cement is discovered. If we penalize an industry for making something the world wants, they will simply pack up their bags and move to some place where they can operate unfettered by restrictions.

Two sectors of commerce that are officially exempted from the Kyoto Protocol are air and marine transport. That is because, once again, there is no alternative to air travel or surface transport of goods across the oceans, and it would be counterproductive to put a carbon tax on something for which there is no replacement. Air travels accounts for 3% of all the greenhouse gases emitted into the atmosphere. There are ways of pushing efficiency levels of air travel, but this is a focus of airline manufacturers anyway, who are keen to reduce fuel used per passenger mile. The marine sector might benefit from new technologies, but these will be implemented by decree or economics.

Here is a depressing thought: growing food produces greenhouse gases. You should pause here and think for a second, because there is more bad news. Growing food for the desperately poor produces lots of greenhouse gases. If that does not quite get you, think about this: the desperately poor grow food in the areas most likely to be flooded when global warming takes hold and ocean levels rise. The gas we are referring to is methane, the second most important greenhouse gas. Earlier, we stated that CO_2 accounts for 60% of the warming potential of greenhouse gases. Methane is estimated to contribute a further 15–20%. The problem with methane is that its impact on global warming is 20 times that of CO_2,[1] but limiting methane emissions is much more problematic than simply reducing the burning of fossil fuels.

Methane drifts up into the atmosphere primarily through natural sources, but in recent years levels derived from anthropogenic sources have been rising. The natural sources of methane now account for only 32% of total methane emissions; of this wetlands account for 24%, and the remaining 8% comes mainly from lakes, rivers and oceans.[2] Anthropogenic sources of methane account for the other 68% of the total emitted into the atmosphere every year. The largest percentage of methane is produced by fossil fuels (20%), closely followed by 16% produced by enteric fermentation mainly by cattle. The rest of the accountable methane emissions are produced by flooded rice paddies (10%), biomass burning (6%), landfills (6%), animal waste (6%) and domestic sewage (4%).

Clearly we can control only the anthropogenic sources, and so the greenhouse gas warriors have targeted four areas for methane emission reductions: fossil fuels, enteric fermentation, rice farming and waste management. We can understand their concern with all these sources of

[1]   This is called the global warming potential, which will be discussed later in the chapter; more detail can be found in the glossary.

[2]   Adapted from Bachelet and Neue, in press; Bouwman 1989; IPCC 1992; Khalil and Shearer, in press; as presented in Heinz-Ulrich Neue, *Methane Emission from Rice Fields*.

methane, with the exception of rice farming, which provides the basic staple food to the world's poor. As a percentage, the amount of rice grown and then sold to second or third parties is minute. Most of the rice produced today is planted by subsistence farmers, who cultivate the crop in order to feed their families.

Nevertheless, the US Department of Agriculture is working on ways to limit methane emissions from the rice paddies of Asia. Their research has shown that draining the rice paddies periodically, which aerates the crop's roots, slows the production of methane from the fields. This has been proven in laboratory conditions, but in the real world rice paddies are flooded by monsoon rains and the water is kept there because there is no other available method of irrigation. Over 50% of the world's population relies on rice as the staple for their diet, and for many of them rice constitutes up to 60% of their calorific intake. The method of flooding paddies helps to prevent soil erosion and also increases yields. The alternatives, which include growing rice only in upland areas, produce lower yields and more frequent crop failures.

The amount of methane produced by the fossil fuel industry is double that emitted from all the rice paddies in the world. Methane is the prime component in natural gas, and where there is coal or oil, there are often large deposits of gas. The gas is captured and piped to urban areas for commercial and residential use. In the process, there is normally leakage from the pipes, a problem that is seldom mentioned by the major gas producers. Leakage from pipelines in the USA and western Europe is normally minimal, but the older Soviet pipelines that feed into the EU are much less efficient. These are being replaced, but the process takes time and money. Methane trapped within coal seams is normally released into the atmosphere during the process of mining. All coal mines monitor methane, as it is explosive in concentrations between 5% and 15%. This methane is pumped out of the mine and vented into the atmosphere. Older, abandoned mines emit methane regularly through vents or the soil strata.

During the process of digestion, methane is produced by livestock, and the amount emitted into the atmosphere corresponds directly with the number of animals raised by the world's farmers. Scientists are exploring ways of changing the diet of cattle in order to reduce the amount of methane produced. In particular, US scientists have been exploring ways of storing manure in oxygen-free environments to reduce build-up of the gas. Interestingly enough, they have discovered that this gas is produced in greater volumes in higher-temperature areas.

For the most part, we cannot reduce methane, except by sealing old mines and using better means of transporting natural gas. The other ways in which methane escapes into the atmosphere are perhaps preventable, but we cannot morally disrupt the lives of subsistence farmers for our own benefit.

We also cannot allow carbon credits to be granted for controlling the agricultural emission of methane. If the US Department of Agriculture finds a way to do this without disrupting the food chain of the developing world, then the effort should be applauded but treated as a humanitarian gesture, not a commercial venture.

While naturally occurring gases account for most of global warming, the man-made gases are thousands of times more toxic, but luckily occur in much smaller quantities. Compounds such as methane and CO_2 have natural lives. They exist in the atmosphere for a time but degrade over the course of years. If we stopped emitting CO_2 and methane right now, the problem of global warming would instantly begin to resolve itself. Man-made gases are in a super league all by themselves. They are stable gases, and it is estimated that they will survive in the atmosphere for thousands of years. To be more specific, PFCs have a probable life in the atmosphere of 7000–10 000 years. From our perspective, looking forward perhaps 100 years, these gases create an irreversible problem, and their control is arguably of much more importance than that of naturally occurring gases.

The first man-made chemicals that entered the public consciousness were chlorofluorocarbons (CFCs). These gases came to the public's attention in the late 1980s as they were recognized as one of the main gases responsible for the depletion of the ozone layer over the South Pole, which allowed greater levels of ultraviolet light into the lower atmosphere. CFCs were primarily used in refrigeration units. A replacement gas was found and a program was instituted that drained off CFCs from discarded refrigeration units. CFCs were banned globally under the terms of the Montreal Protocol and amended acts to the US Clean Air Bill in 1990.

Many of the replacement gases used in refrigeration units manufactured globally since the ban on CFCs have been equally damaging to the environment and have been subsequently banned under the terms of the Copenhagen Amendment to the Montreal Protocol.

The Kyoto Protocol has targeted three specific classes of man-made gases: HFCs, PFCs and SF_6. These are described as "classes" of gases because, with the exception of SF_6, they can take many forms. HFCs, for instance, come in the form of HFC-23, HFC-143a, HFC-4310mee and many others, while PFCs can travel under the names of CF_4 and C_6F_{14}. Notice that all the man-made gases we are discussing – CFCs, PFCs, HFCs and SF_6 – have an "F". This is the magic ingredient, fluorine, that creates so much trouble. If these gases were used only in refrigeration units the problem would be easier to solve, but they crop up in a whole host of industrial processes.

Let us start with one of the worst offenders, PFCs. These are compounds that contain only carbon and fluorine, hence the name C_6F_{14} for example.[3] As far as we know, they are not ozone depleting, but they are powerful greenhouse gases.

[3] If you want to picture one of these compounds, imagine a similar hydrocarbon and then replace the hydrogen atoms with fluorine atoms, so methane (CH_4) becomes CF_4.

One of the sources of this gas is the aluminum industry. There is a particular electrolytic smelting process called the Hall-Héroult method. Without getting into details of the approach, the anodes are made of graphite (carbon), and the electrolyte contains fluorine; during the process, PFCs are formed at the anode. The USEPA estimates that the annual PFC emissions from aluminum smelting in the USA is around 2700 tons, which is equivalent to 18.5 million tons of CO_2.

PFCs are also used in the computer industry. To give one application here, hard disks need lubricating, and the lubricant needs a carrier, a solvent if you like. And the best solvent is a PFC because of its properties.

PFCs are probably the most stable substances known to man, hence their extraordinarily long life in the atmosphere. It is because of this stability that PFCs have been proposed for use in fire suppression, as vapour blankets for flammable materials for example.

HFCs are less stable than PFCs. Whereas PFCs contain only carbon and fluorine, HFCs also contain some hydrogen.[4] HFCs are used in refrigeration, air cooling systems and in making foam.

Sulfur hexafluoride (SF_6) is a heavy, inert, nonflammable gas with a lifespan estimated to be in the order of 3000 years. Unlike PFCs and HFCs, it comes in just one variety, SF_6, but it has a range of properties that make it useful in a variety of industries. Probably its most important characteristic is that it is a very effective electrical insulator, and is used instead of oils or air in high-voltage systems. It allows for more compact and reliable equipment, in particular circuit breakers and high-voltage switch gear. In smelting operations, the fact that SF_6 is both inert and five times heavier than air means that it is ideal as a cover gas to exclude oxygen from the process and hence prevent oxidation. This is particularly important in magnesium foundries.

The industry that uses all these man-made gases in some form is the

[4]   For PFCs, we said that every hydrogen atom of a hydrocarbon is replaced by a fluorine atom. For HFCs, only some of the hydrogens are replaced.

semi-conductor industry, where the gases are used for plasma etching and cleaning. The gases are critical to the industry because, at the moment, there are no known substitutes. All the alternatives that have been developed have also proved to be greenhouse gases.

Remember it was CFCs that were originally banned for depleting the ozone layer. These were then replaced with PFCs and HFCs. While these newer gases appear to have no effect on the ozone layer, they do cause global warming. The fact is that these gases are designed to be stable, which is one of the problems: when they escape into the atmosphere they do not degrade.

Man-made gases are insidious, and every effort must be made to assure that their effects are limited. A cure may exist for them in the future by emitting another gas that negates the effect they have on the problem. That may be wishful thinking, but if such a cure were found, that should certainly qualify for greenhouse gas credits.

Global warming is impacted by a number of gases, and if we want to understand the problem fully, we have to know how much the various gases impact upon the problem. From a financial perspective, we have to also know how credits can be obtained by reducing these substances. Some of these gases are very damaging, and are recognized as being significantly more important than CO_2. The idea behind calculating global warming potentials (GWP) is that it creates a sort of exchange rate between the various gases. So, for example, one ton of methane is worth the same as 21 tons of CO_2. This means that we can now put a price on releasing a ton of methane into the atmosphere: if a CO_2 credit is trading at \$15/ton, then the "value" of a ton of methane is \$315. Obviously, the only reason we are interested in the price of a ton of a particular gas is that the gas contributes to global warming, and so to work out the exchange rate between the gases, we need to look at the potential impact these gases can have on the upper atmosphere. And this is precisely what the GWP aims to do (see glossary for details).

The starting point in understanding the potential damage of each gas is not a simple matter of quantifying the amount of longwave radiation the substance reflects in the atmosphere, as judged by laboratory experiments. These gases can act directly and indirectly on the problem. A direct effect is straightforward, that is to say that the gas independently reflects longwave radiation in the atmosphere at a certain rate. An indirect effect means that the gas combines with other gases in the upper atmosphere and increases the effect, or it mutates over the course of time into another gas, or it changes the lifespan of other gases in the atmosphere.

11

KYOTO HAS NO SOUL

Global warming is, above all, a moral issue. It will hurt the poorest of the world in the worst places of the world. Rising sea levels and dramatically intense tropical storms will wipe out entire ways of life in Africa and south-east Asia. While the middle classes can at least pack up their bags and move to high ground, the poor will not have any such luxuries. It takes a certain level of arrogance to dismiss the issue and consign the powerless classes of the world to an unacceptable fate. We are clearly not environmentalists, as we value life on earth more than we value earth itself, but we accept that this issue is unique. Although it goes against our grain to preach an environmentalist's mantra, in this case saving the most desperate of the world requires that we do our utmost to preserve the environment in which they live. There comes a point in all our lives where we have to make a stand, and at this point in the history of our world, we have to collectively conclude that it would be immoral to shirk our responsibility to those we will never meet or know.

The good news is that we believe we will solve the problem without putting ourselves through a century of self-flagellation. Of the many scientists and analysts working on the problem, the most admired is probably Dr James Hansen of the NASA Goddard Institute for Space

Science. Not only is he considered to be one of the top environmental scientists in the world, he is singularly credited with bringing the issue to the attention of the world. Like us, Hansen is an optimist. He believes this problem can be resolved much sooner than many others in the scientific community estimate. His prognosis is based upon extensive analysis of the upper atmosphere, which has demonstrated a recent downturn in carbon concentrations, probably the result of a greater natural uptake in the oceans. Hansen feels that a significant effort to reduce methane emissions, as well as to cut out the minor greenhouse gases, would significantly slow the effects of global warming. His most recent article has been somewhat misinterpreted by the conservative press, who are twisting his views to justify an abandonment of the effort entirely. Hansen states clearly that the efforts to reduce particulate pollution and slow down the emissions of CO_2 must continue. He goes on to state that it is highly unlikely that the process will continue on until 2050, because at that point the issue will be resolved. We agree with him on his prognosis, but think he is in fact being too conservative. We think most of the problem will be solved by the year 2020. We are not saying that the problem of global warming will go away, but by that time we will have done just about everything possible to reduce the global emission of greenhouse gases, short of capping every volcano in the world. In two decades, the model for change will be altered fundamentally, and the rate of global warming will be slowed to such an extent that the issue will not be considered life-threatening to the planet.

Solutions to society's problem can be driven by either the political hierarchy or grass roots action from the people. As a rule of thumb, the former seldom works and the latter invariably succeeds. Right now, we are in the position where the politicians of the world are essentially working in a vacuum trying to determine a definitive policy that will satisfy everyone and still resolve the problem. Eight years after Rio, and three years after Kyoto, the policy makers are still in discussions trying to sort out the definition of a forest and whether nuclear power should be considered a viable option. Controversy still surrounds the potential US decision to buy so-called "hot air" from Russia, and it has yet to be determined whether turning the soil less frequently reduces emissions. The reality is that trying to solve any complex problem and imposing a host of laws and regulations on an unwilling public only creates resentment. The laws will either be flouted or exploited for any loopholes. For any initiative as bold as this, it is important that the people believe in the spirit of the law rather than just being forced to follow the letter. To be blunt, the Kyoto Protocol is sterile. This is not to say that it is worthless, but simply that it has no soul and does not yet represent a real solution. The solution must come from the people, but for this to happen the message must first be spread by the politicians and the press.

It is of paramount importance that the political risks involved with implementing a solution be taken into account. We cannot suddenly impose an agenda on an unwilling and unaware world. A new cost structure that penalizes people for their successes in life will not be politically acceptable. Imposing solutions, pricing products out of the market, and throwing down a whole new gauntlet of taxes will only ensure that the process of change is halted instantly. America is the most important participant in this process, and if it is not on board, the Kyoto Protocol will be worthless. Americans have federal elections every two years, and each vote is really a judgement on the economy that the government has delivered the people. Jimmy Carter and George Bush were two US presidents that got a quick education in the motivation of the American voter. Both were good men, but unfortunately they presided over economies stuck in the doldrums through little fault of their own. If the next president deliberately imposes a tax structure so onerous that it plunges the nation into a recessionary spiral, he or she will be lucky to complete his or her term in office.

Once the voters of the world get behind the issue, the policy makers, environmentalists and government ministers can happily pack their bags and go home because the battle will be won. The people of California have demonstrated what they can do when they are motivated to clean up the air they breathe. Individuals have ultimate power. They can force manufacturers to create clean products, and force the flows of investment into innovative solutions. When the individual is motivated, the era of false solutions will end immediately and the practical business of stopping global warming will really begin.

Global warming is not the fault of industry; it is the fault of all the individuals in the world who breathe, heat their houses or take a car or bus to work. We tell industry what to produce and we buy their products, and it is no great challenge to tell them to do something differently. Industry will have to be responsible for finding innovative solutions to this problem, but it is the responsibility of the public to set up a reward system that benefits companies that do this soonest and produce the best results. Industry has no responsibility to take this problem on its back and resolve it until it is told to do so by the voters.

When they do decide to vote on the issue, the public will also be the ones that decide which alternatives they want. In the cold light of day, the concept of planting forests to "capture" carbon will be scrutinized and found to be what it is: a false science that may actually make the problem worse. Windmills and all the other renewable energy options will be looked at in a real economic sense, and only those options that can consistently supply the backbone of a national grid, and are cost effective, will be put into place. Nuclear energy may be a politically sensitive option, but if the new generation of safe, cheap and easy-to-install reactors is the only carbon-free power option available, a new consensus will build up that will eventually overcome environmental concerns. The fuel cell industry is in its infancy, but with the investment that would be necessary to begin mass manufacture of these products, there is no reason that we cannot retire the internal combustion engine over the course of the next two decades. Ethanol is the only green fuel we have that can really be put to use in power transportation. The USA and Brazil produce it already in massive quantities, and production is becoming much more efficient. Within this decade, it is conceivable that a good proportion of the private car fleet in Japan, the USA and Europe could run on a carbon-neutral fuel.

We already know which solutions will work best, because we can see where the money is going. This money is not being driven by global warming concerns, but by environmental concerns due to local smog pollution and a natural drive by industry to create more efficient solutions to problems. The invention of the two-piece aluminum can, which reduced the amount of metal used in production to one-eighth of that of the old style, was not driven by environmental concerns. It was a new technology borne out of the desire to create greater efficiencies and lower costs. The same can be said for the fuel cell. If the need to reduce local pollution did not exist, the product would have been developed anyway. The pebble bed modular reactor was not designed as a direct result of the Kyoto Protocol. It was funded because it really does work and is a cheap and safe way of adding clean power quickly to a national grid. Voter pressure that results in legislative action, such as California's Clean Air Act, only sets up a reward system for positive change, which speeds up an existing process. It creates a new impetus to throw money at real solutions, but it will not create an environment where it is feasible to put money into projects that will never work. The laws of economics are absolute: money will always be attracted to real investments that offer real returns. The best we can do as individuals is to streamline the process, which is what the voters of California have done.

The causes of global warming are far more complex than we have indicated, although some of the solutions are much simpler. We have concentrated on the underlying problem, the emission of CO_2, and the reasons are obvious: not only does CO_2 contribute the largest percentage to global warming, but it is also linked to our lifestyles. To address this problem will require industry to come up with alternatives and for us to change our lifestyles. While this may take a while to happen, there is another area that is much easier to focus upon and tackle – man-made gases. Most of these are created by mankind for use in industry. The computer industry relies on certain environmentally harmful man-made gases for the manufacture of circuit boards and other components. With proper supervision, safety procedures can be put in place to prevent the escape of these gases into the atmosphere, and with financial incentives in place, less harmful replacements can be found. The removal of non-CO_2 gases from the atmosphere will have a direct bearing on the timing of climate change, and by acting quickly, we can buy time to ensure that the alternatives we need for reducing CO_2 can be implemented.

The new economy we will create in the process of halting global warming will be radically different from the carbon-based economy that drove growth in the twentieth century. A carbon-free economy will place more value on technology rather than on the fuel that powers it. Wealth will diminish in the OPEC states and other energy-producing countries. If there is a move to ethanol, agricultural production in the tropics will increase dramatically, as will wealth generated from the export of carbon-neutral fuel. Exploration for lower-grade carbon fuels will become uneconomic, and greater efficiencies in energy use should help to restore the balance of trade in the USA and other energy-importing countries. A move to carbon-free nuclear energy, or hydro and geothermal energy, should stabilize the price of electricity, allowing for continued economic growth.

The health of the citizens of the world should also improve as rates of cancer deaths due to particulate pollution decrease. The threat of spreading tropical diseases and parasites would also be halted as temperatures stabilize. Local air pollution will diminish considerably, and even metropolises like Mexico City would become habitable again. The damage brought about by acid rain will cease, and forests in the USA, Canada, northern Europe and the rest of the polluted world should begin to thrive again.

This sounds like an idyllic world and a wonderful place in which to live. This may not be how it turns out, though. To make this happen requires a collective will, and this will not be mobilized until the political leadership of the developed nations stands up and explains why our entire biosphere is at risk. The factors that prevent this issue from becoming a major concern to the majority of the population are simple. Global warming is invisible, and its progress is too slow to measure with any accuracy. Mankind will not suddenly wake up, see global warming one morning, and demand political action to stop it. But we do have the intelligence to comprehend an abstract problem, and we can understand the moral implications if the developed world pretends the issue does not exist.

What happened at Kyoto was important because at least it got the ball rolling and is beginning to stimulate investment. This investment has to be poured into technological innovation, instead of a panoply of false solutions. Planting trees, fertilizing the ocean and putting a windmill in everyone's backyard will do nothing to stop the process of climate change. These false solutions are blinkered at best, and at the extreme can be viewed as cynical exploitation of regulatory loopholes.

We believe there is an infinitely better approach than any of those mentioned above. In our world, the battle against global warming will be fought in the corporate finance departments of investment banks, in the offices of venture capitalists, and in the research and development departments of the world's major corporations. The complex system of trading carbon credits will only be worthwhile as a vehicle to streamline the investment process into real solutions, and by the year 2020 they will be collectors' items because they will be out of circulation. The carbon market may be active for the next two decades, but it is really only a sideshow. In our world, capitalism will sort out the problem, and it will be done at a price we can afford and a speed we can manage.

We are rationalists and believe that the simplest way to stop global warming is to stop burning fossil fuels, or burn them in a way that limits the amount of CO_2 that enters the atmosphere. We are never going to be totally clean, and we do not really have to try. We do not have to give up barbecuing hamburgers over a charcoal fire or mowing the lawn every weekend. If there is a reward system set up that provides an incentive for technological solutions, money will just pour more rapidly into the industries that are working on the problem. There is a big school of thought that exists in the world that actually fears the idea of technology being released to solve the problem. This is not our fear, but our hope.

We believe in the future of the fuel cell and think it will change the way we power our cars, trains and ships. We believe that the energy companies will develop new solutions that allow the burning of fossil fuels without the production of greenhouse gases. We believe a new generation of nuclear power will continue to provide the world with cheap electricity. We really have no need for new types of genetically modified trees that eat carbon and walk themselves into a biomass plant to be turned into green fuel. We do not need to cover the oceans' surfaces with algae, nor do we have to destroy every scenic vista with 300-feet-high windmills. We do not need to dam every river, or cover the Sahara in solar panels. We do not need to turn in our cars and be issued government-approved bicycles.

Our world will let us sit outside for coffee and have a conversation unhindered by the roar of traffic. We will be able to hop in the car and drive two blocks to the supermarket without becoming overwhelmed with guilt. We will be able to turn on the microwave knowing that we are getting cheap and clean power, and we will be able to turn up the refrigerator to make sure the beer is so cold that it's just on the verge of freezing. We will also be able to look outside the window on Christmas Eve knowing that, if everything is perfect, it just might snow.

GLOSSARY

Acid rain   Literally, rain that is acidic in nature. As with all acids, it may burn what it comes into contact with. Acid rain destroys forests, kills life in lakes, and gets into the water table, causing problems for other vegetation. The main culprit for causing acid rain is burning *fossil fuels*. Amongst the gases that are emitted are sulfuric and nitrous oxides, which rise in the air and mix with water vapor, at which point they turn into sulfuric and nitric acids, hence creating acid rain.

Activities implemented jointly (AIJ)   See *Flexibility Mechanisms*

Annex I parties   Refers to the countries that are listed in Annex I of the *United Nations Framework Convention on Climate Change* (UNFCCC). The initial objective was to take emissions back to 1990 levels by 2000. New targets for 2008–2012 were then assigned to these countries under Annex B of the Kyoto Protocol. Annex I countries are: Australia, Austria, Belarus, Bulgaria, Canada, Czech Republic, Denmark, Estonia, Finland, France, Germany, Greece, Hungary, Iceland, Ireland, Italy, Japan, Latvia, Lithuania, Luxembourg, Netherlands, New Zealand, Norway, Poland, Portugal, Romania, Russian Federation, Slovakia, Spain, Sweden, Switzerland, Turkey, Ukraine, UK (Great Britain and Northern Ireland), the European Union (EU) and the USA.

Anthropogenic   From the Greek word *anthropos*, which means "man". In the context of global warming, this is used to differentiate emissions produced by man rather than nature.

Alliance of Small Island States (AOSIS)   Global warming and sea levels are a particular problem for low-lying nations, which are vulnerable to a rise in the level of the ocean. These nations tend to be small, and have little influence on international policy. In order to communicate more effectively their position, they have formed the AOSIS. There are 42 members and observers, which include American Samoa, Antigua and Barbuda, Bahamas, Barbados, Belize, Cape Verde, Comoros, Cook Islands, Cuba, Cyprus, Dominica, Federated States of Micronesia, Fiji, Grenada, Guam, Guinea-Bissau, Guyana, Jamaica, Kiribati, Maldives, Malta, Marshall Islands, Mauritius, Nauru, Netherlands Antilles, Niue, Palau, Papua New Guinea, Samoa, Sao Tome and Principe, Seychelles, Singapore, Solomon Islands, St Kitts and Nevis, St Lucia, St Vincent and Grenadines, Suriname, Tonga, Trinidad and Tobaga, Tuvula, US Virgin Islands, and Vanuatu.

Atmosphere   Layers of air that bound the earth as a result of gravity. The two key layers are the *troposphere* (at the bottom) and the *stratosphere* (on top). The troposphere extends for around 12 km and holds the clouds, weather patterns and the gases that give rise to global warming. The stratosphere contains around 25% of the total mass of the atmosphere, but because it is further away and the gravitational pull is weaker, it is a much thicker layer and extends to about 50 km above the earth. The ozone layer is held in the stratosphere.

Banking, emissions   If a country or company produces less emissions than it is entitled to, the surplus balance can be banked and used in future periods. This concept was established under the *United Nations Framework Convention on Climate Change* (UNFCCC).

Barrel   Traditional unit of measure for oil that comes from the early days of the oil industry when oil was transported in old wine barrels. A full barrel actually contains around 49 gallons, but because of spillage, it became common practice to count a barrel as 42 gallons.

Baseload   The amount of electricity that is always required per day, irrespective of the changing demands due to time of day and time of year, e.g. the electricity that runs your alarm clock, fridge etc.

Berlin Mandate   Adopted at the first *Conference of the Parties* (COP) meeting in Berlin in 1995, this launched the talks that led to the Kyoto Protocol.

Biomass   Strictly speaking, this is a measure of the amount of stored energy in dry organic material and living organisms, but it is generally used more loosely to mean a type of renewable energy. It includes pretty much anything we can burn that is natural, and that is not included in the "fossil fuel" category. So, for instance, a tree is biomass. Although we used the idea of burning in the definition, this does not mean that we are necessarily going to burn it; we may recycle it in other ways, as paper for example. The important point is that biomass is considered to be "carbon neutral", in that burning a tree simply puts back into the atmosphere the same net amount CO_2 that the tree absorbed when it was growing.

Biomass burning   The systematic clearing and burning of vegetation so as to prepare the ground for agricultural purposes.

Carbon cycle   The movement of carbon between various reservoirs. Generally, we think of the four main carbon reservoirs as being the ocean, the atmosphere, terrestrial biosphere (essentially organic life) and the sediments (mainly *fossil fuels*). The movement of carbon between these reservoirs can be classified in various ways, but for our purposes it is helpful to split it into fours categories. The first is the flows that result from organic life in the form of respiration, photo-synthesis and decomposition. Historically, this is a continuous and relatively stable flux, although it has been disturbed by deforestation. The second category is the movement between the atmosphere and the ocean, again a stable, continuous flow. The final natural source comes from volcanic activity, a more erratic type of emission that can occasionally upset the balance. The real change to the carbon cycle, though, is the burning of fossil fuels. This is a relatively recent activity, and the only one that releases carbon from the sediments. Scientists are uncertain as to how the carbon cycle will be effected by *global warming*.

Carbon dioxide (CO_2)   The key *greenhouse gas*, and the cause of 60% of the *global warming* effect. The principal cause is the burning of *fossil fuels* (hydrocarbons). The carbon in the fuel combines with the oxygen from the air, producing CO_2, which floats up into the atmosphere. See also *Carbon cycle*.

Chlorofluorocarbons (CFCs)   A family of compounds that contain chlorine, fluorine and carbon atoms. They are man-made chemicals designed for use in the refrigeration industry and in aerosol cans. They were one of the main culprits identified with depleting the ozone layer, and were phased out under the 1987 Montreal Protocol.

Clean development mechanism (CDM)   See *Flexibility Mechanisms*

Conference of the Parties (COP)   In this context, "Conference" means "association" rather than a meeting. The COP refers to the countries who have signed the *United Nations Framework Convention on Climate Change* (UNFCCC). The COP meetings are referred to as "sessions", hence the expression "the sixth session of the Conference of Parties". This group of countries form the supreme body of the convention, which meets each year to discuss implementation of the convention. The first meeting (COP-1) took place in Berlin in March/April 1995; COP-2 was in Geneva in July 1996; COP-3 was in Kyoto, December 1997; COP-4 was in Buenos Aires in November 1998; COP-5 was in Bonn in November 1999; and COP-6 is due to take place in The Hague in November 2000.

Earth Day   Founded by Gaylord Nelson, then a senator from Wisconsin, the first Earth Day was in the USA in 1970. The aim was to get people from all backgrounds to demonstrate about environmental issues. In the event, 20 million people turned out, which led to the creation of the US Environmental Protection Agency and the passing of the Clean Air Act, the Clean Water Act, and the Endangered Species Act. Since then Earth Day has become a global event.

Emissions trading   See *Flexibility Mechanisms*

Flexibility Mechanisms   These are a way of giving parties a little flexibility in achieving their targeted cuts. In the run-up to the Rio Summit, a mechanism known as Joint Implementation (JI) was introduced. This subsequently found its way into the text of the *United Nations Framework Convention on Climate Change* (UNFCCC), although the hard decisions were postponed until the first *Conference of the*

Parties (COP) meeting. Since then, other mechanisms have been introduced, but it is still not 100% clear as to what the precise guidelines are. Broadly speaking, there are two forms of Flexibility Mechanism. The first group are project-based and aim to make changes that reduce emissions where reductions would not otherwise occur. The second group revolves around trading the credits. A clean development mechanism (CDM) is a project in which an *Annex I country* invests in a non-Annex I country in order to reduce emissions. The resulting "certified emission reductions" can be used by the investor to assist in meeting their reduction commitments. CDM is a modification of the original JI for projects in non-Annex I countries, and was introduced in the *Kyoto Protocol*. JI, or Activities Implemented Jointly (AIJ), is still the name of the mechanism that would be used if the project involved an Annex I investment in another Annex I country. Emissions trading allows countries to buy and sell emissions credits. The objective is to increase flexibility and hence reduce the overall cost of implementing the targets. Within countries, schemes are also being set up to allow companies to trade amongst themselves. It is then up to the individual countries to decide on the level of international trade that is allowable.

Fossil fuels   A term used to describe oil, coal and natural gas that can be burnt to produce heat, power or propulsion. The word "fossil" comes from the fact that they are all the fossilized remains of carbon-rich plants and animals that died millions of years ago; this differentiates them from other "renewable" forms of fuel. The problem is that fossil fuels are hydrocarbons, which release CO_2 into the atmosphere when burnt.

Framework Convention on Climate Change   See *United Nations Framework Convention on Climate Change*

Fuel cells   A fuel cell is essentially the same as a battery. The key difference is that the fuel is replenished so it does not wear out. The "fuel" in this case can be any number of hydrogen-rich compounds. The goal is to use pure hydrogen, but at this stage of development the fuels that are being considered are gasoline, natural gas, methanol and ethanol. The main use for fuel cells will initially be for powering cars, but as the technology develops further, they could be used to replace many other forms of power.

Global warming   A loose term used to cover all aspects of the global warming problem. In other words, the level of warming, and the effects on the earth and its inhabitants. It is taken as read that this is a result of emissions created produced by mankind.

Global warming potential (GWP)   This measures the warming produced by one ton of a gas divided by the warming produced by one ton of CO_2 over a 100-year period. The period of 100 years was chosen by the *Intergovernmental Panel on Climate Change* (IPCC) and has become the accepted standard. The following table shows the GWP for the main gases, as calculated by the IPCC.

	Gas	**GWP**
Naturally ocurring gases	CO_2	1
	Methane	21
	Nitrous oxide	310
Man-made gases		
HFCs	HFC-23	11 700
	HFC-125	2800
	HFC-134a	1300
	HFC-143a	3800
	HFC-152a	140
	HFC-227ea	2900

	Gas	GWP
Man-made gases		
HFCs	HFC-236fa	6300
	HFC-4310mee	1300
PFCs	CF_4	6500
	C_2F_6	9200
	C_4F_{10}	7000
	C_6F_{14}	7400
	SF_6	23 900

Source: IPCC 1996.

Greenhouse effect   An accumulation of *greenhouse gases* in the lower atmosphere. The sun emits heat in the form of shortwave radiation, which passes straight through the gases. The earth, on the other hand, re-emits the heat in the form of longwave radiation, which is partially trapped by the gases. This is a natural phenomenon that traps heat in the earth's atmosphere and helps sustain life. The potential problem comes when we burn *fossil fuels*, so increasing the concentration of the gases and thus warming the earth further.

Greenhouse gases (GHGs)   There are a large number of GHGs, but the six that are targeted by the *Kyoto Protocol* are carbon dioxide (CO_2), methane (CH_4), nitrous oxide (N_2O), perfluorocarbons (PFCs), sulfur hexafluoride (SF_6) and hydrofluorocarbons (HFCs). The first three of these are naturally occurring gases and, according to the United Nations, are the largest problem. The other three are man-made gases. In addition to these, another important culprit is, surprisingly, water vapor.

Hot air   The economies of some countries, notably Russia, were running at full steam in 1990, which is the base year for the targeted cuts.

With the collapse of these economies, they will not only be able to meet their requirements without investment, but they will have spare "credits" available. These credits are referred to as "hot air", and are currently a cause for concern, especially amongst environmental groups who point to this as a major loophole in the *Kyoto Protocol*.

Hydrocarbons   Compounds that are principally made up of hydrogen and carbon, a family that includes the *fossil fuels*.

Intergovernmental Panel on Climate Change (IPCC)   Established in 1988 by the World Meteorological Organization and the United Nations Environment Program (UNEP). Its task is to review the scientific evidence available relating to climate change. It has become the international authoritative body on climate change and undertakes work as requested by groups associated with the convention.

Joint Implementation (JI)   See *Flexibility Mechanisms*

Kyoto Protocol   Agreed at COP-3 meeting in Kyoto in December 1997, this is an extension of the *United Nations Framework Convention on Climate Charge* (UNFCCC). Under the Kyoto Protocol, *Annex I countries* aim to cut emissions of the various *greenhouse gases* from 1990 levels. The first commitment period is 2008–2012, by which time countries have to make their targeted cuts. The targets levels are shown in the table below. Note that some countries are allowed to increase their emissions from 1990 levels, for example Australia can increase by 8%.

Country	Percentage change required
Australia	8
Austria	−13
Belgium	−7.5
Bulgaria*	−8
Canada	−6
Croatia*	−5
Czech Republic*	−8
Denmark	−21
Estonia*	−8
Finland	0
France	0
Germany	−21
Greece	25
Hungary*	−6
Iceland	10
Ireland	13
Italy	−6.5
Japan	−6
Latvia*	−8
Liechtenstein	−8
Lithuania*	−8
Luxembourg	28
Monaco	−8
Netherlands	−6
New Zealand	0
Norway	1
Poland*	−6
Portugal	−27

Country	Percentage change required
Romania*	−8
Russian Federation*	0
Slovakia*	−8
Slovenia*	−8
Spain	15
Sweden	4
Switzerland	−8
UK	−12.5
USA	−7
Ukraine*	0

* Countries that are undergoing the process of transition to a market economy.

Methane (CH_4)   This is one of the three naturally occurring *greenhouse gases*, and is second only in importance to carbon dioxide (CO_2). In terms of its heating potential, it is 21 times as effective as CO_2. It is commonly known as natural gas, and is often associated with deposits of oil. As a general rule, methane is created when matter decays in the absence of oxygen, for instance in flooded rice paddies, where the roots get little or no oxygen, methane is given off. Similar emissions are associated with other wetland areas. This also explains why it also comes as a by-product of digestion, and leaks from landfill sites.

Missing carbon sink   We can estimate what goes into the atmosphere and what is absorbed, but there appears to be some carbon missing. This is referred to as the "missing carbon sink".

Nitrous oxide (N_2O)   The third of the three naturally occurring *greenhouse gases*. Humans create nitrous oxide emissions by burning the dirtier fossil fuels, such as coal, and through the use of nitrogen fertilizers.

Ozone   The ozone layer resides in the upper atmosphere and absorbs harmful ultraviolet radiation. It is an unstable molecule made up of three oxygen atoms. In the 1980s, it was discovered that the release of *chlorofluorocarbons* (CFCs) into the atmosphere destroyed the ozone. As a result, CFCs were banned under the Montreal Protocol.

Pollution   A broad term covering various types of damage to the air quality. The three aspects that have become main issues are *acid rain*, *ozone* depletion and *global warming*.

Protocol   An extension to a convention. It adds to or refines commitments already in the convention, and must therefore be ratified separately.

Ratification   To become a party to either a convention or a protocol, the country must first sign and then ratify it. Ratification usually requires approval from the a governmental body.

Renewable energy   Wood is said to be renewable in that as the tree grows it absorbs carbon dioxide (CO_2). When the wood is burnt, the CO_2 is released back into the atmosphere. The fuel itself can be renewed by growing another tree. This category generally includes solar, geothermal, wind, biomass, ocean/wave, and hydro energies. We can also say that ethanol produced by fermentation is a source of renewable energy.

Sequestration   Used to describe the act of removing and storing carbon dioxide. Often used in relation to carbon *sinks*, such as forests.

Sink   The precise definition has yet to be agreed, but in essence this is a reservoir that takes carbon dioxide out of the air, for example wetlands, forests and vegetation. These are important since they are included in the protocol as a way in which countries can meet their targets: they count as negative emissions.

Smog   Derived from the words "smoke" and "fog", this is the layer of polluted air that hangs over many cities. It is the result of the release of sulfuric oxides when *fossil fuel* is burnt into damp air. While this has been dealt with in most cities, it has been replaced by another type of pollution referred to as photochemical smog. This is created by a complex reaction between nitrous oxides and hydrocarbon emissions from cars, and gives rise to a yellowish haze that hangs in the air.

Solar energy   Energy derived from the sun. Most solar energy is captured by heating up water, which is then used for heating, hot water, or to produce steam to turn turbines to generate power. Direct production of electricity via photovoltaic cells is very expensive.

Stratosphere   See *Atmosphere*

Sustainable development   A loose term that recognizes that there needs to be a balance between the short-term demands and the longer-term implications. In other words, is the development or consumption sustainable over the long term?

Troposphere   See *Atmosphere*

United Nations Framework Convention on Climate Change (UNFCCC)   Signed in June 1992 at the Earth Summit in Rio by 154 countries. The aim was to bring the emissions from developed countries down to 1990 levels by 2000. The agreement also set up a framework through which the parties can meet on a regular basis.

Whole World's Watching, The   The chant of the protesters at the 1968 Democratic National Convention in Chicago.

Printed and bound by CPI Group (UK) Ltd, Croydon, CR0 4YY

09/06/2025

14685964-0001